SAINT OSCAR ROMERO

SAINT OSCAR ROMERO
Pastor, Prophet, Martyr

KERRY WALTERS

franciscan
media
Cincinnati, Ohio

Cover and book design by Mark Sullivan
Cover image © Brother Octavio Duran, OFM

Copyright ©2018, Kerry Walters

ISBN 978-1-63253-265-7

Published by Franciscan Media
28 W. Liberty St.
Cincinnati, OH 45202
www.FranciscanMedia.org

Printed in the United States of America.
Printed on acid-free paper.
18 19 20 21 22   5 4 3 2 1

To the good people of Holy Spirit parish

Each time we look upon the poor, on the farmworkers who harvest the coffee, the sugarcane, or the cotton, or the farmer who joins the caravan of workers, looking to earn their savings for the year...there is the face of Christ.

The face of Christ is among the sacks and baskets of the farmworker; the face of Christ is among those who are tortured and mistreated in the prisons; the face of Christ is dying of hunger in the children who have nothing to eat; the face of Christ is in the poor who ask the church for their voice to be heard. How can the church deny this request when it is Christ who is telling us to speak for him."[1]

—SAINT OSCAR ROMERO

CONTENTS

Journey to Sainthood

"Carry on, always seeking truth, justice, peace, and freedom. Christ will give us strength so that we won't lose heart along the way."[1]

Oscar Romero, Archbishop of San Salvador, was gunned down on March 24, 1980, while celebrating Mass. Over the next few days, his body lay in state in the cathedral where he had so often preached. Thousands of mourners filed past his coffin, many of them *campesinos,* landless peasants and field workers, who had traveled miles to be there.

They hadn't come just to pay their respects to a Church dignitary, although that was certainly part of it. They came because they loved Romero. During the three years he served as their archbishop, they knew him as a father who stood between them and a death-dealing government. Now that he was gone, they not only felt orphaned, they were terrified.

Pleading flyers pasted on the cathedral walls said it all: "Archbishop, talk to God for El Salvador!"[2]

Thanks in large part to the biopic *Romero* released by the Paulist Fathers in 1989, many people know something about the extraordinary journey of this pastor, prophet, and martyr canonized by Pope Francis in October 2018. He has become a symbol for our time of a Christian hero who dared all, risked all, and sacrificed all—but a sacrifice of victory, not defeat—for the sake of love.

No one but God could have seen that Romero, a timid, introverted, and very traditional priest would evolve into the heroic saint he became. His origins were humble and his performance as a seminary student unremarkable. For the first twenty-five years of his ordained life, he was a conscientious pastor and diocesan administrator. But nothing extraordinary stands out. His understanding of his priestly calling was solidly traditional: celebrate Mass, administer sacraments, organize catechism classes, collaborate with Catholic relief agencies, and offer spiritual counsel and consolation to the people he shepherded.

Nothing particularly heroic.

Over the next seven years of his life, Romero served primarily as a diocesan bureaucrat with few pastoral duties and became an auxiliary bishop of San Salvador. During this period, he gained an unsavory reputation as a lackey of the right-wing politicians and wealthy landowners who used the nation as their own personal estate. He became involved in one acrimonious feud after another with progressive clergy, especially Jesuits, whom he believed had gone off the rails.

The source of the conflict was Romero's resistance to the liberation theology agenda that emerged from a groundbreaking 1968 conference of Latin American bishops at Medellín, Colombia. Liberation theology offered a fresh way of reading the Gospels and a new focus for evangelization that emphasized material as well as spiritual salvation and sought to empower victims of poverty and injustice. In El Salvador, these were the *campesinos* who drudged under miserable conditions for barely subsistent wages. Romero pitied their plight, but worried that advocates of liberation theology, zealous as they were to redress injustice, fixated on political and economic activism at the expense of dedication to Christ. During these years, he never missed an opportunity to assail them, often intemperately, in speech and writing.

Not much evidence of saintliness here.

And yet the Spirit blows where it will, moving each heart in unfathomable ways. Even as Romero fulminated against the "Red" priests of El Salvador, the oppressiveness of his nation's political and economic structure and the uptick in violence became increasingly apparent to him and burdensome to his conscience. Gradually, over his last five years of life, and especially following the 1977 government-sanctioned murder of his friend Rutilio Grande, a Jesuit who lived and worked with *campesinos,* something that had been stirring in Romero finally clicked.

He realized that fidelity to Christ required more than he had hitherto given, that the Church and her priests are called to care for society's most vulnerable members even if that means defying unjust legal, economic, and social structures that oppress them. He perceived that this was not a politicized repudiation of the Gospels or of Christ, but a return to both by a Salvadoran Church that historically had lost its way by aligning itself with the powerful against the powerless. Romero came to see that *salvación integral,* the total salvation of body and soul advocated by liberation theologians, was entirely consistent with the teachings of the Lord.

> The human progress that Christ wants to promote is that of whole persons in their transcendent dimension and their historical dimension, in their spiritual dimension and their bodily dimension. Whole persons must be saved, persons in their social relationships.... This is the integral human salvation that the Church wants to

bring about—a hard mission!... [This is] the revolution of Christ's love. [3]

A "revolution of Christ's love" perfectly expresses the new vision that transitioned Romero from a conscientious but unremarkable (and, at times, curmudgeonly) priest to a heroic prophet. A revolution motivated by the power of love instead of arms, a revolution that seeks not the overthrow but the conversion of society: This became Romero's focus during his final three years as archbishop of San Salvador.

For the ruling elite, conversion meant the softening of their stony hearts and an embrace of the biblical truth that all people are equally beloved by God and equally deserving of the world's resources. For the *campesinos,* conversion meant an awareness that their misery was not the will of God, that Christ suffered along with them, and that the Gospel could empower and liberate them. For the Church, conversion meant being a source of material and spiritual hope for the hungry, thirsty, forlorn, naked, sick, and oppressed. "The hope that our Church encourages," said Romero, "is neither naïve nor passive. It is rather a summons from the word of God for the great majority of the people, the poor, that they assume their proper responsibility.... And it is support, sometimes critical support, for their just causes and demands. The hope that we preach to the poor is intended to give them back their dignity, to encourage them to take charge of their own future." [4]

Romero's newly embraced prophetic ministry was dismissed by critics then and now as political ideology masquerading as piety. He was accused of being a Communist, an agitator, a Soviet stooge, a gullible fool, imprudent, unintelligent, and a bad priest. The calumny hurled at him soured his relations with the Vatican, leading to humiliating curial scolding during his lifetime and stone-walling on his canonization after his death. But Romero was clear in his own mind and conscience that he was doing Christ's work, not playing power politics. In a homily delivered in November 1979, he insisted, as he would numerous times, that calling out injustice is an "incarnation" of God's Word in the suffering of the people, not an exercise in political partisanship or demagoguery.

> We not only read the Bible, we analyze it, we celebrate it, we incarnate it in our reality, we want to make it our life. [Our goal is] to incarnate the Word of God in our people. This is not politics. When we point out the political, social, and economic sins in the homily, this is the Word of God incarnate in our reality, a reality that often does not reflect the reign of God but rather sin. We proclaim the Gospel to point out to people the paths of redemption.[5]

A few people who knew Romero suggest that Fr. Grande's murder was a road-to-Damascus experience which instantaneously trans-formed him from a timid and traditional priest into a prophet-hero proclaimer of Christ's revolution of love. The supposed sudden conversion is sometimes called the "Rutilio miracle." Although it makes for high drama—it's the centerpiece of the Paulist Fathers' biopic—the Rutilio miracle account ignores the complexity of Romero's spiritual journey. Moreover, he denied that Grande's murder spontaneously changed him. Instead, he saw the tragedy as a tipping point in his steadily growing awareness of what God was calling him to do.

One way to appreciate the dynamics and cumulative effect of Romero's spiritual journey is to view it through the lens of folk-lorist Joseph Campbell's analysis of the hero's journey. Campbell argues that there is a transcultural and transhistorical pattern common to all stories about heroes found in myths, legends, fairy tales, and even religions. Whether in the ancient Sumerian epic of Gilgamesh, the saga of the Arthurian knights, the *Star Wars* films, Tolkien's *Lord of the Rings* trilogy, or, for that matter, the Gospel accounts of Christ's life, death, and resurrection, all heroes traverse a predictable series of developmental stations that draw them ever-deeper into an awareness of their true identity and mission. They leave the comfortable and stable familiarity of home to venture out into an alien and frightening world where they battle with monsters. They are eventually slain along the way, often symbolized by a "going-under" into "graves" of water or subterranean caverns. But they rise again, phoenix-like, rejuvenated and sure of who they are and what they're called to do. They then return home, to the place where their journey began, empowered to rescue and serve those they left behind.

Each of the journey's way stations is crucial to the heroic quest. The pilgrim must leave home, run up against unexpected and discombobulating challenges, and die to his or her old self. There are no shortcuts, no quick fixes, no sudden transformations.

Romero's own journey from priest to prophet to martyr follows this pattern. The comfortable and safe home he left, a departure that took him several years, was his traditional view of what it meant to be a priest. The monsters he encountered and battled along the way were, initially, of his own making—liberation theology's new mode of evangelization—but later were the very real ones of state-sponsored terrorism and institutionalized injustice. Finally, slain to his old self by the shock of Grande's murder, Romero rose from the grave—Grande's grave, as it turned out—to take on the mantle of heroic prophet and offer the opportunity for total, integrated salvation to all Salvadorans, the oppressed first, but their oppressors as well. No one is outside the reach of the returned hero's beneficence. Even those who do evil are embraced if they repent and convert.

And yet the story of Romero's heroic journey seems to end anti-climactically for the obvious reason that he was killed—not the symbolic dying to self which is one of the stages of the hero's journey, but an actual snuffing out of his life by an assassin's bullet. Moreover, twelve brutal years of civil war erupted in El Salvador immediately after his death. Doesn't this suggest that Romero's journey ended in failure? Doesn't his martyrdom reveal him to be a vanquished hero and silenced prophet?

No. The priest's task is to bring the people to God, and the prophet's to bring God to the people. The martyr's unique role is to display a devotion to God and the Kingdom so boundlessly loving that it reignites in the rest of us a faith that may have grown tepid or even cold. We look to the martyrs to remind us that some things are worth sacrificing our lives for, but that the love which motivates us to make those sacrifices is more powerful than death itself. This is the great truth embodied in the resurrection, and every individual martyrdom, including Romero's, is a reflection of it. Martyrdom is a victory, not a defeat, a loud proclamation of God's glory, not a silencing of God's Word, an affirmation, albeit a bittersweet one, that human wickedness can never win in the end.

Therefore, St. Oscar Romero, priest, prophet, and martyr, lives on. Liberation theologian Jon Sobrino once described him as a living Gospel, a piece of Good News to the world's poor that continues to sustain all who suffer from oppression or who struggle, sometimes against heartbreaking odds, for justice.

Romero also sustains us through his heavenly intercessions for peace and justice in the world's nations. This, too, is part of his heroic journey, for a hero, remember, works to save those he leaves behind.

In being martyred, Romero rose again. His name and what he stood for are now familiar to people around the globe. Sobrino notes that everywhere he goes in the world, Latin America, Europe, Canada, Asia, or the United States, people want him to speak about St. Oscar. "In Tokyo, New Delhi, and in so many other places, I have been struck by how much Archbishop Romero means to Christians, Marxists, Buddhists, and Hindus. 'I have some bad news for you,' a European told me one day. 'Archbishop Romero does not belong just to Salvadorans any more. He belongs to the world now.'"[6]

Indeed he does.

CHAPTER ONE

Childhood

"I...I would like to be a priest!"[1]

Within hours of Archbishop Romero's assassination, a shocked and grieving Jon Sobrino, one of Latin America's leading liberation theologians, sat down to compose a memorial to the man he once had dismissed as a malleable pawn of El Salvador's wealthy and politically powerful elite.

"The first thing I want to say of Archbishop Romero," wrote Sobrino, "is that he had a profound faith in God. We know of the devotion, felt not feigned, with which he spoke of God in his homilies. We know of his spirit of meditation and his simple, down-to-earth prayers. For him, to speak with God was something as straightforward and routine as life itself."[2]

Sobrino was right. Romero, like all saints, was a man so deeply committed to prayer that it could almost be said his entire life was one long conversation with God. Even as a child, he displayed a devotion to prayer that was disarmingly precocious. It was one of the most common recollections of those who knew him when he was a youngster.

Oscar Romero was born in the early hours of August 15, 1917, in Ciudad Barrios, a town in the highlands of northeastern El Salvador, located in the department of San Miguel, one of the nation's fourteen administrative districts. Nestled under the

Cacahuatique mountain range, the town bore the same indigenous name as the mountains surrounding it until rechristened in honor of Gerardo Barrios, a politician and coffee baron who served as the nation's president until deposed and executed in 1865. Ciudad Barrios claimed him as a native son, although several other municipalities in San Miguel did so as well.

The remote town, just ten miles south of the Honduran border, was inaccessible except by horseback or foot during Romero's childhood. Most of its roughly one thousand inhabitants made their living from subsistence and cash-crop farming. Located three thousand feet above sea level, the cool climate was particularly suitable for growing coffee, and many townspeople either owned or rented terraces on the mountain slopes to make a few extra *colóns* by growing and cultivating coffee.

Despite its remote location, the town was economically stable. No one was especially wealthy, but most families managed to make ends meet. Merchants sold goods, the streets were cobbled, there was a telegraph and post office, and the plaza was illuminated by carbide lamps. Still, the household into which Romero was born was sometimes financially pinched, especially after his father's death.

Romero's mother, Guadalupe de Jésus Galdámez, was a native of Ciudid Barrios, and she inherited one of those hillside plots as well as a tiled house in the town square that had running water, an indoor lavatory, and a small enclosure for a cow and some chickens. His father, Santos Romero, was an outsider, born in Jocoro, a town in another department. After a rather itinerant young adulthood, he came to Barrios in 1910 to be its telegrapher and postmaster, and soon wooed and married Guadalupe. Together they had eight children, one of whom died young. Oscar was their second eldest. There was also an illegitimate daughter sired by Santos who remained in Barrios her whole life.

Curiously, Oscar was nearly two years old before he was finally baptized in May 1919 by Fr. Cecilio Morales. It is not clear why his parents waited so long. Santos, quick-tempered and impatient, seems not to have been particularly religious, but nonetheless taught Oscar simple prayers when the boy was old enough to learn them. Guadalupe, on the other hand, was especially devout, leading the family in rosary devotions every night. One explanation for the late baptism might be that the toddler came down with a life-threatening illness that made the long-deferred sacrament urgent. Years later, a family friend recalled collecting medicinal herbs for the severely sick boy. But his memory may be confused about dates, because a cousin recalls that when Oscar was seven he suffered a serious illness, perhaps polio, which left him paralyzed and speechless for a period.

All the Romero children helped out with household chores: working the plot of land, milking the family cow, and collecting eggs from the hens. Oscar, perhaps because he was too sickly to do a lot of heavy work, was recruited to assist Santos in receiving and transmitting telegrams. Oscar's elder brother Gustavo was also a helper, and eventually replaced their father for a time as the town telegrapher.

Reminiscences about the childhoods of saints are always a bit suspect, because the temptation is to filter them through a pious lens. But many people, family and acquaintances alike, remembered Oscar as a quiet boy, serious nearly to the point of solemnity. A couple of his siblings recall that "as a boy he seemed a little sad." He "always turned inward, thought too much."[3] In all likelihood, this introspection was encouraged by his bout of polio.

He was also intensely devout from an early age. "Of all of us," remembered one of his brothers, "he was probably the one who prayed the most." Even in play, Oscar's piety came through. "What games did he play? Well, he seemed to get the most fun out of doing processions. He'd put one of mother's aprons over the top of him and go around on the streets calling out to the other kids, pretending he was already a priest."[4]

A story that Romero often told about an event in his childhood testifies to how young he was when he felt the stirrings of a call to holy orders. The bishop of his diocese, Juan Antonio Dueñas, who a few years later would send eighteen-year-old Oscar off to Rome to study for the priesthood, made an episcopal visit to Ciudad Barrios. Oscar, decked out in brand-new clothes for the occasion, apparently followed him everywhere he went. Finally the bishop, probably out of a mixture of exasperation and amusement, asked the boy what he wanted to be when he grew up.

"Well, I...I would like to be a priest!"

According to Romero, the bishop jabbed him in the forehead with a finger and declared, "You, my boy, are going to be a bishop!"

Years later, in telling the story, Romero pointed to his forehead and remarked, "I can still feel the touch of his finger right here." [5]

A youngster who dresses up as a priest, leads playmates in pretend religious processions through town, and decides at a prepubescent age that God has destined him for the priesthood is alarmingly close to coming across as a prig. But helping to soften Oscar's precocious childhood piety was delight in the pageantry and excitement of the circus. "Oh, and the circus!" recalled his brother Tiberio. "He would die to go to the circus. He never missed one! You know, the tightrope walkers doing those balancing acts way up there on the wire.... And the clowns! Circuses were his greatest joy." [6] Both the piety and his enthusiasm for circuses remained with Romero throughout his life.

There was another thing that delighted the young Oscar and softened what might otherwise have been a streak of exaggerated solemnity: music. Santos was something of an amateur musician, and taught his son to play the bamboo flute, an instrument common in the El Salvador highlands, and to read music. Later, during his seminary studies, Romero picked up the piano and harmonium. Music remained one of his great delights, and his tastes were generously eclectic, ranging from classical to folk. As archbishop, he often asked his driver to play marimba music on the car radio.

Early on, Oscar also showed a love of learning, but there were few educational opportunities in Ciudad Barrios. The town school offered only the first three grades. After he had completed them, Oscar's parents let him study privately for a couple years under the school's teacher. But that ended when the boy was eleven or twelve. Santos then reckoned it high time for his son to close the books and learn a trade. So he apprenticed him to the local carpenter.

Given Oscar's hope to be a priest, as well as the high regard in which the Church was generally held by Salvadorans at this time, Santos's decision to nip his son's vocation in the bud is startling. Perhaps it was prompted by worry that the family could not afford more education for Oscar, or maybe the decision was simply motivated by Santos's relative indifference to the faith. At any rate, the apprenticeship seemed to spell an end to the boy's dreams of becoming a priest. It must have been a terrible letdown for him.

Nevertheless, fellow apprentices remember him as a dedicated and skilled student of carpentry. The craftsman to whom he was apprenticed thought him the best of his wards (or at least said so afterward when Romero was a bishop), and for years proudly showed to visitors a mahogany joiner's gauge that Oscar had made while serving under him. For his part, despite his dashed hopes, Oscar must have been more or less content working for the master carpenter because as an adult he always took time to visit him whenever he returned to his hometown.

The call to the priesthood, however, remained with him. After work, he almost always stopped in the town church for devotions before returning home, and his brothers remembered their annoyance at his frequent risings in the middle of the night to pray. Others, including the diocesan vicar general and the mayor of Ciudad Barrios, also sensed that young Oscar was meant for something other than carpentry. After some lobbying on their part, possibly done at Oscar's request, Santos finally gave in and agreed to let his son attend minor seminary in San Miguel. To allay the financial burden on the family, the bishop agreed to pick up part of the boy's tuition, with Santos doing his part by donating coffee beans to the seminary. Oscar helped out by working odd jobs, including one summer spent laboring in a gold mine. But most of his wages that summer went to medical expenses. Guadalupe had never fully recovered from the birth of her eighth and final child, and the bills for her treatment had piled up.

Oscar left for the seminary in 1930 when he was thirteen years old. It was quite a move for the introverted boy. San Miguel was a full day's horseback ride from Ciudad Barrios. Unlike the pleasantly cool mountainous climate that Oscar was used to, the climate of San Miguel, located as it is in the lowlands, was hot and humid. Moreover, the town was huge by El Salvador standards, boasting nearly twenty thousand residents.

When he arrived at San Miguel, Oscar joined some forty other seminarians, aged thirteen to eighteen, who lived and studied on a horseshoe-shaped campus. Each of them was assigned a plot of land to grow vegetables for the kitchen, and they were also expected to care for the dozens of fruit trees on the grounds. These policies not only expressed the seminary's conviction that idle hands were the devil's tools, they also helped to keep the perpetually financially strapped institution afloat.

The days there for Oscar and his classmates were pretty much alike. The boys were awakened each morning at 5:30, attended Mass an hour later, then breakfasted and were in classes for eight hours. Schedules allowed time for meals and recreation, but in fact there was little leisure and less freedom in the seminary. For all practical purposes, the boys lived like strictly regimented monks.

A number of photos of Oscar survive from his time at the minor seminary. Two in particular, marking the beginning and the end of his years there, stand out. In the first, taken when he was thirteen, he is seated with fellow students, dressed like them in a black cassock, hands resting on his knees. His eyes stare intently at the camera, but the rest of his face is strangely, almost bovinely, expressionless. It takes a moment to realize that the youngster's gaze is directed more inwardly than outwardly, suggesting that his interior world is more real for him than the exterior one. The second photo, taken in his final year at the seminary, shows the same unsettling combination of intensity and expressionlessness.

The introversion captured by these photographs characterized Romero from an early age and remained with him his entire life. As a priest, bishop, and archbishop, he was always on the go, working tirelessly to serve God and his people. The inward gaze, in other words, didn't inhibit him from participating in the outer world. This is because it betokened first and foremost the deeply prayerful approach that Romero as a boy, adolescent, and adult brought to his everyday activities. Far from interfering with his practical ministries, his interior world fueled them and sustained them.

But introversion sometimes can also lead to unhealthy self-absorption, perfectionism, and hypochondria, and Romero struggled from tendencies to all three throughout his life. He was forever drawing up prayer, devotional, study, and work schedules so demanding that no mortal could possibly keep up with them. He was often preoccupied with his health, physical as well as mental, consulted psychiatrists and psychologists as well as medical practitioners, and occasionally suffered physical collapses brought on by stress and worry. Perfectionist that he was, he was often disappointed in his efforts and accomplishments and pushed himself to the point of exhaustion. This in turn occasionally made him impatient and quick-tempered like his father, Santos.

Life at the minor seminary encouraged Oscar's native affinity to prayer and introspection. The school was operated by the Claretians, an order founded in the mid-nineteenth century, whose professed members are especially called to work with the poor and sick, and who share a special devotion to the Immaculate Heart of Mary. During his time with them, Oscar grew to love this devotion and remained faithful to it for the rest of his life.

His years in the minor seminary were rewarding and happy. Years later, Romero described the seminarians and their Claretian mentors as a genuinely close family. Although he visited his biological relatives regularly (he also sent them his dirty laundry each week to clean and return), he found a sense of fulfillment and solidarity with his seminary classmates that was lacking back in Ciudad Barrios.

Although introverted, Oscar seems to have enjoyed a certain degree of popularity, particularly after he was befriended by Rafael Valladares, a brilliant young man born into one of El Salvador's coffee-rich families who was everybody's favorite at the school. His classmates even gave Oscar the affectionate nickname of *cabeza de sungano,* "mophead," because his hair was so thick and bushy. Rafael immortalized the moniker in a bit of doggerel written for the school newsletter:

> Like a fragrant bush
> In Ciudad Barrios I was born and bred.
> And here in San Miguel
> I grow into a handsome mophead. [7]

Although Oscar's personal life at San Miguel was happy, a national tragedy struck during his second year there that couldn't have failed to infiltrate even the closed-off and safe environment of the seminary.

The nation into which Romero was born is the tiniest in Central America, barely 82,000 square miles, no larger than Massachusetts. During his childhood, it also became the most densely populated one. In the generation before his, between 1880 and 1920, the number of Salvadorans more than doubled, and it grew even more rapidly during Romero's lifetime. This created a huge labor force of landless peasants, or *campesinos,* ripe for exploitation by wealthy landowners.

During Romero's lifetime, the *colón* was El Salvador's currency. But the nation's wealth was coffee beans—"red rubies," as Romero sometimes called them, a reference both to the color the beans took on when they ripened and the riches they brought to the *cafetaleros,* or coffee growers. Throughout the 1920s, as worldwide markets for coffee expanded and most of El Salvador's arable land was bought up and cultivated by the nation's wealthy elite, its economy boomed. The landowners, of course, were the primary benefactors. But even so, some of their good fortune trickled down to the landless peasants who tended and harvested the beans, slightly improving their living conditions.

Then the bottom fell out. The worldwide depression that hit in 1929 slashed the demand for coffee. Sales tumbled and landowners, struggling to hang onto whatever margin of profit they could, reduced the already pitiable wages of their workers from about two dollars a day to less than thirty cents.[8] By 1931, as hard times really settled in, the landless poor were lucky to find employment at all, and even then the pittances they earned were frequently gobbled up by company stores owned by their employers. Because the wealthy landowners refused to give up the cash crop of coffee for food crops that could be consumed domestically, hunger and illness partnered with poverty to create abominable living conditions for *campesinos.* Those who could tried to supplement their income and diets by growing a bit of food. But the soil available to them was of poor quality and little yield.

On January 22, 1932, the peasants' misery and growing resentment erupted in a rebellion in the nation's southwest, a region hit particularly hard by bad weather and sparse harvests. El Salvador's Communist party, led by Agustín Farabundo Marti, collaborated in the uprising, as did many of the region's indigenous Pipils.

The rebellion barely got off the ground before it was over, crushed in less than a week by the ruling oligarchy that pulled out all the stops to quell it and maintain the status quo. The Salvadoran military was let loose on the *campesinos*, and the killing continued for a solid month, resulting in the death of some thirty thousand peasants, Pipils, and Communists, including Marti. The bloodletting, which came to be called *la Matanza*, "the Slaughter," was so fierce that it reduced the *campesino* population by a shocking 2 percent.[10] It signaled to the nation's landless peasants as well as to the political left that the military, political, and moneyed elites who ran El Salvador would tolerate no dissent.

Despite the minor seminary's cloister-like atmosphere, it is likely that Oscar and his classmates followed the horrific events of *la Matanza* in newspapers, radio reports, and word of mouth. Images of slain rebels and lurid accounts of executions, all intended by authorities to underscore the cost of resisting power structures, must have burrowed deep into his psyche. In a fundamental way, both the injustice and oppression that led to the rebellion and horrible killing that followed in its wake defined the economic, political, and cultural climate of the El Salvador in which Romero would live and die. It also eventually influenced how he came to see his duty as a Christian leader.

CHAPTER TWO

Romanità

"The Lord has inspired in me a great desire for holiness."[1]

Oscar graduated from San Miguel minor seminary in 1935 when he was eighteen years old. In the normal course of events, he would've either remained there to begin priestly formation—the seminary was both a minor and major one—or been sent by his bishop to San José de la Montaña, the Jesuit-run major seminary in San Salvador, the nation's capital.

But things weren't normal. The same economic depression that led to the collapse of the nation's coffee market also helped spark civil war in Spain, and most of the Spanish-born Claretians who staffed the San Miguel seminary were called back to their mother country to replace clerics who had been killed in the struggle. This left the institution too understaffed to offer adequate priestly training, and Salvadoran-born diocesan clergy were already too overworked to fill in the gaps. So Oscar found himself in limbo for a few months until his bishop, Juan Antonio Dueñas—the same bishop who had poked him on the forehead in Ciudad Barrios—finally made the decision in 1937 to send him to San José. It's likely, however, that he received some one-on-one instruction after graduating from San Miguel, because he entered the major seminary credited with a year of theological study.

During his first few months in San Salvador, tragedy struck at home: His father, Santos, died in August, one day after his fifty-fourth birthday and one day before Oscar's twentieth. Santos had been in a bad way for several years. During the economic crisis that ruined the coffee economy and erupted in *la Matanza,* he'd managed to lose the small landholding inherited by Oscar's mother, Guadalupe. To make matters even worse, the land had been seized by the godfather of one of Oscar's brothers after Santos had defaulted on a personal loan. Humiliated by the loss and racked with financial worries, Santos took to drink and let himself go.

At around the same time, Guadalupe, already in frail health, seems to have suffered a stroke that left her right side partially paralyzed. Oscar worried mightily about how his semi-invalid mother and younger siblings would get by after his father's death, and he resolved to support them as best he could when he became a priest. In the meantime, two of his brothers took on financial responsibility for the family.

Given the difference in their temperaments, the relationship between Oscar and Santos was a complicated one. But it's clear that the son was saddened by the loss of his father. He gave voice to his grief in a prose poem written a few months later.

> The sun goes slowly to its setting, the afternoon grows languid. His eyelids, drooping sadly are robbing the day of its splendor, its joy, its light. How sad is the evening!
>
> Everything, my God, speaks of sadness, of weeping.
>
> But, oh, within my breast today is an eventide more sorrowful.... My father is dead! Dear Father, I who each evening turned my gaze to the distant east, sending you my loving distant thought, would think of you on the

porch of the home I remembered, would see you turning
your gaze to the west where your son was....[2]

Romero went on to recall how his father taught him simple prayers
and surprised him with toys "made with [his] own hands." The
poem's tone is adolescently lachrymose and even slightly mawkish,
but there's no reason to doubt either the grief or the affection it
expresses.

Oscar's stay at San José de la Montaña seminary was short-
lived. After only a half-year there, he was informed that Bishop
Dueñas had managed to obtain scholarships for him and two of
his fellow seminarians, Alberto Luna and Mauro Yano, to live
at the Colegio Pio Latino Americano in Rome and study at the
Gregorian University. Founded in 1858 and staffed by Jesuits,
the Colegio was devoted to preparing Spanish- and Portuguese-
speaking men from Central and South America for the priesthood. The three youths would join Rafael Valladares, the slightly
older student who had been with them at San Miguel and who
had written the poetic tribute to Oscar's unruly hair. Valladares
had been a seminarian in Rome since 1934.

Valladares and Romero, who were friends at minor seminary
and remained devoted to one another until Valladares's premature
death in 1961, were an odd couple. (A second unlikely friendship would develop years later between Romero and Jesuit priest
Rutilio Grande.) Romero came from a rural and not terribly
well-off family, while Valladares was the son of a wealthy land-
owner and the nephew of Bishop Dueñas. Romero was temper-
amentally insecure and anxious. Valladares, a beneficiary of the
many privileges that the Salvadoran aristocracy enjoyed, had
the self-confidence that comes with belonging to a privileged
elite class. He had an outgoing personality and was a sparkling

conversationalist, while Romero tended to be uncomfortable and wallflowerish in large crowds.

Romero and his three companions boarded an Italian liner, the *Orazio,* in late 1937, making a stop at a port in Venezuela to pick up a few more seminarians on their way to Rome. It was the first venture from his family for one of them, and he was miserably homesick. Romero did his best to cheer him up by cracking Spanish and Italian puns.

Otherwise, however, Romero was the most serious of the dozen or so Rome-bound seminarians, coming across to some of them as stuffy and stiff. He declined their invitations to watch movies shown during the voyage, preferring instead to pace the deck praying his rosary. Several priests were also traveling to Rome aboard the *Orazio,* and he assisted them two or three times a day at Mass. The same combination of intense interiority and aloofness apparent in his minor seminary photographs was on full display.

After a voyage of eleven uneventful days, the seminarians arrived in the Eternal City. It would be Romero's home for the next six years. The importance of Romero's formation there can't be overstated. He fell under the influence of all things Roman— or at least all things Vatican—an attitude traditionally labeled *romanità.* Rome instilled in the young Salvadoran a deep fidelity to the institution and hierarchy of the Church, unwavering devotion to its doctrines and traditions, and a deep appreciation for its spiritual traditions, particularly as expressed by the Jesuits. As he wrote two decades after his return to El Salvador, "The privilege of studying in Rome was valuable not so much for the scholarly aspect as for the moral support of a priestly education completed in the Roman setting. Rome is the most beautiful symbol and synthesis of the Church."[3]

Much has been made of an alleged conversion that took place in the final three years of Romero's life which threw his lifelong dedication to the Church in question. But this has been vastly overstated. Romero remained a creature of *romanità* to the end. He always considered himself a stalwart son of the Church, even though his understanding of what that entailed certainly did undergo a change in his final decade. To overlook this by transforming him into a man at war with the Church is to distort who he was.

One clear indication of Romero's traditionalism was his lifelong devotion to Pope Pius XI, sometimes called "the last imperial pontiff," who still occupied Peter's throne for the first year and a half of Romero's Roman period.

Romero's admiration for Pius was fourfold. In the first place, he was impressed by the pope's deep dedication to the overseas mission of the Church. During his pontificate, Pius did more than any of his predecessors to encourage evangelization in developing nations and the ordination, whenever possible, of native priests. Even as a young man, Romero sensed that poor and distant countries like his own had been neglected by a Eurocentric curia and that consequently both Catholicism and priestly formation for men in Latin America, his own part of the non-European world, had suffered.

Romero also approved of Pius's deep concern for social justice— yet another indication that his final years as Archbishop of San Salvador were more of a culmination than a break with convictions he had held for years. In his 1931 encyclical *Quadragesimo Anno,* Pius reaffirmed the social teaching pioneered in Leo XIII's *Rerum Novarum.* Pius took on both liberal and conservative political economists, arguing against both that although there is indeed a right to private property, it is one which must always be weighed against the requirements of the common good. Subsequent popes such as John Paul II and Francis have affirmed the same principle.[4]

Pius's forward-looking attitude when it came to science and communication technology also impressed Romero. The pope refurbished the Vatican Observatory, encouraged revisions in seminary curricula, modernized the extensive Vatican library, and founded the Pontifical Academy of Sciences the year before Romero arrived in Rome. Although Romero was a conscientious and even bookish student, he never considered himself an intellectual. But he was convinced that Christianity had nothing to fear from the social and natural sciences, and in fact could learn from them. In his final pastoral letter as archbishop of San Salvador, for example, he defended the analytic value of Marxist social science methodology while rejecting its materialist ideology.

As priest, bishop, and archbishop, Romero took full advantage of new technology in spreading the Gospel. He was almost certainly inspired by Pius, who did likewise. In 1931, the pope installed Vatican Radio in Vatican City, and was the first pontiff to regularly broadcast over the airwaves. In the early days of his own ministry, and again when he was named bishop of Santiago de María in 1974, Romero attached a loudspeaker to beat-up vehicles so that he could preach to all and sundry as he drove through the countryside. He also regularly broadcast radio addresses and sermons throughout his entire career. Although a somewhat timid public speaker in his youth, he matured into a fine preacher whose wit, charisma, and authenticity captivated audiences. In his three years as archbishop, it was said that two-thirds of the nation regularly tuned into his Sunday homily broadcasts.

Finally, what impressed Romero about Pius XI was his

willingness to stand up to tyrants in hateful and death-dealing regimes. Although the pope worked with Italian prime minister Benito Mussolini in 1929 to arrive at the Lateran Treaty which granted sovereignty to Vatican City, Pius also issued an encyclical three years later blisteringly critical of Italian fascism. He launched an even fiercer denunciation in 1938 when Mussolini, under pressure from Hitler, began persecuting Jews.

Similarly, although he signed a concordat with Germany in 1933 in the hope of containing Soviet expansion, Pius issued no fewer than thirty-four public rebukes of the Nazis over the next three years. He finally broke with them altogether in 1937 when he ordered German priests to read from their pulpits his encyclical *Mit Brennender Sorge,* a no-holds-barred denunciation of Nazism as antithetical to Christianity. Like Pius, Romero would later be willing to work with power brokers in his own nation so long as there was the chance of converting them and mitigating their oppressive political and economic institutions. But in his final years he fearlessly spoke truth to power when pastoral efforts at changing the hearts of the elite failed.

Romero's devotion to Pius, the pope who stood up to repressive regimes and who insisted that no one would laugh at the Church as long as he was pope, never wavered. "In Rome," the future archbishop later wrote, "I had to live through the drama of the Church facing the totalitarianisms of Hitler and Mussolini. I learned from the imperial Pius XI the boldness to confront those in power fearlessly."[5] On his final journey to Rome, just weeks before his assassination in 1980, Romero remarked after praying at Pius's tomb, "This is the pope I most admire."[6]

Once immersed in his studies, Romero quickly acclimated to his new life. Along with the 150 other Latin American seminarians living at the Colegio, he regularly assisted at Mass, observed designated prayer periods throughout the day, and attended classes at the Gregorian. Meals were eaten in silence while seminarians listened to readings from spiritually edifying works.

But there were also vacations and holidays that sometimes included class trips to the seaside. Romero, a particularly strong swimmer, challenged his fellow students at least once to a race, the designated finish line being a rock jutting above the waves some distance from the beach. Reaching it ahead of everyone else, as he knew he would, he triumphantly perched atop it—only to make the painful and humiliating discovery that it was covered with sea urchins whose spines stung him pretty badly.

His swimming skills aside, what struck his fellow students most about Romero was the same buttoned-down seriousness he had displayed in the minor seminary and on board the *Orazio* when he'd preferred rosary devotions to movie-watching. As one of them described him,

> He had a deliberate bearing, like one who is not hurried to arrive because he knows he will get there. With other persons he was peaceable, calm—like one who knows that life has to be taken as it comes—rather quiet, a bit shy. His conduct was irreproachable; I never knew of anything that would lessen this judgment. He was observant of the regulations, pious, concerned for his priestly training at every aspect. With others, he could make friends and was regarded by us who were his friends for his simplicity and desire to help.[7]

Pope Pius XI died in February 1939. Romero and his entire cohort of seminarians attended the funeral, and he remembered touching "with an indescribable emotion" the dead pontiff's hand.[8] Six months later, Europe was at war as Hitler's Wehrmacht raced to conquer its neighbors and impose the policy of ethnic cleansing that would horrify the world. Nine months after that, on June 10, 1940, Italy joined the war as Germany's ally. Romero and a few friends heard the news over an outdoor loudspeaker as they strolled in one of the city's piazzas.

War meant that Rome was a potential bombing target, and the Jesuit administrators of the Colegio, anticipating the coming danger, began sending seminarians back to their home dioceses whenever it was safe to do so. The Latin American students were stuck in Europe, at least for the foreseeable future, because German U-boats made transatlantic voyages risky. Romero, who had been in the habit of writing his mother long monthly letters, was now reduced to communicating with her in notes of no more than twenty-five words conveyed by the Red Cross.

As Italy's food supplies were increasingly siphoned off to feed soldiers, hunger became a problem in the city of Rome, and the seminarians remaining at the Colegio and Gregorian felt it as well. The two rectors of the Colegio did their best to find food for their wards, sometimes resorting to the black market, sometimes foraging from the city's hundreds of chestnut trees. But still the students were undernourished. One of Romero's classmates recalls that it was an almost daily occurrence for one or another of them to faint from hunger during classes at the Gregorian.

Romero was somewhat accustomed to want and hardship. After all, he'd been born and raised in a nation in which most of the inhabitants were landless *campesinos,* and his own family, although not of the peasant class, wasn't wealthy. But the misery he endured and witnessed in Rome during the war years was a new experience for him. He encountered starving people in the streets of Rome every day begging for whatever food they could get from passersby. On one occasion, he was so touched by the misery of one of them that he handed over a bit of bread he'd been hoarding for himself.

Still, despite his hunger and the tension of wartime, Romero persevered in his studies, taking his licentiate in theology from the Gregorian in 1941. With no way to leave Rome, he continued his priestly formation and was ordained in April 1942 after reaching the canonically required age of twenty-four. He also began work on a doctoral dissertation, choosing as his topic the doctrine of Christian perfection or holiness in the work of a sixteenth-century Jesuit named Luis de la Puente.

In researching his dissertation, Romero studied de la Puente's *Meditations on the Mysteries of Our Holy Faith*, a multi-volume, broadly ranging work that begins with an examination of purgative and illuminative prayer, spiritual exercises that encourage self-examination, contrition, openness to the Spirit, and holiness. De la Puenta's work was attractive to Romero because he found the Jesuit spiritual tradition particularly rewarding. In immersing himself in de la Puenta's writings, especially his biography of Balthazar Alvarez, a Jesuit who served as Teresa of Ávila's spiritual director, Romero discerned, "The Lord has inspired in me a great desire for holiness. I've been thinking of how far a soul can ascend if it lets itself be possessed entirely by God. It is a shame to waste such precious time and such valuable resources."[9]

Dedication to the institutions and traditions of the Church, which is the heart of *romanità*, and the inspiration of Pius XI's courage in standing up to political oppression were two legacies of Romero's sojourn in Rome, although the second took a few years to come to the forefront of his ministry. An ardent longing for holiness is the third, and it sustained the other two, even though it also inflicted on him periodic and unproductive feelings of spiritual and personal inadequacy.

Romero's research for his doctorate was interrupted during the spring and summer of 1943 when Allied bombers finally appeared over Rome. In just a few weeks they flew over five hundred sorties that targeted transportation hubs and factories, killing thousands of civilians. That was enough for Bishop Miguel Angel Machado, who had succeeded to the see of San Miguel two years earlier on the death of Bishop Antonio Dueñas. Despite the hazards of transatlantic travel, he called Romero and Rafael Valladares home, apparently concluding that the Nazi U-boats in the high seas were less dangerous than Allied aerial bombardments.

The two young priests departed Rome on August 16, 1943, a day after Romero's twenty-sixth birthday, on a nonstop flight to Barcelona, a safe haven because Spain was neutral in the war ravaging Europe. From there, they boarded a ship to Cuba, from whose shore they intended to make their way to El Salvador.

The crossing took a couple of weeks and was thankfully uneventful. Their arrival in Havana wasn't. To their dismay, Romero and Valladares found themselves immediately detained by port authorities. Cuba had declared war on the Axis powers almost immediately after the Japanese bombing of Pearl Harbor, and all visitors from Axis nations were considered foreign hostiles. The port authorities who interviewed Romero and Valladares were unimpressed by their protests that they were native Salvadorans and that their only reason for being in Rome had been to study for the priesthood. The two were dispatched in short order to an internment camp, one of several established in wartime Cuba, where they were put to hard labor.

Under the circumstances, things could have gone much worse for them. Even so, they were bad enough. Food and medical assistance in the camp were scarce, and the work was exhausting. Valladares, who was never physically strong, soon became worn down and ill. Fortunately, their ordeal lasted only four months. Some Havana-based Redemptorist priests got word that the two men were fellow clerics and began lobbying for their release. Cuban officials finally agreed to let them leave the country for Mexico, whence they then embarked overland to El Salvador.

They were back in the diocese of San Miguel by New Year's Eve, and Romero traveled shortly thereafter to Ciudad Barrios to celebrate Mass for the first time in his hometown. After an absence of seven years, it must have been a joyous homecoming, despite Guadalupe's ill health and the keenly felt absence of Romero's brother Rómulo, who had died of appendicitis while his older brother was studying abroad.

During this first Mass in Barrios, a second prediction that one day he would be a bishop occurred. A ten-year-old named Moises Gonzalez who was in the church was so moved by Romero's sermon and priestly bearing that he immediately afterward told his grandmother, "I have a feeling that priest is going to be a bishop."

"Oh, so you're a fortune-teller, are you?" she retorted. "What do you know about being a bishop?"

"I don't know about it," Moises said, "but I can imagine."[10]

The boy's confidence in his future would have surprised the young priest. On the eve of his April 1942 ordination, Romero had admitted that he was nervously uncertain about the step he was about to take, especially the vow of lifelong chastity that it entailed. But two years earlier, he had published a piece in the

student newsletter of the Colegio that spelled out his understanding of what it meant to be a priest of Christ, and it was
an understanding that would deepen, despite his pre-ordination
jitters, throughout his career. He couldn't have known just how
accurately this reflection, written when he was only twenty-two,
predicted his own ministry and eventual martyrdom.

> This is your heritage, O priest: the cross. And this is your
> mission: to portion out the cross. Bearer of pardon and
> peace, the priest runs to the bed of the dying, and a cross
> in his hand is the key that opens the heavens and closes
> the abyss...
>
> To be a priest means to be, with Christ, a crucified one
> who redeems and to be, with Christ, a risen one who
> apportions resurrection and life.[11]

CHAPTER THREE

Busy Priest

"What's important is be ready to live the gospel with all
the fidelity we're capable of, with authenticity."[1]

Romero celebrated his first Ciudad Barrios Mass on January 11,
1944, and was consecrated an auxiliary bishop of San Salvador
on June 21, 1970. The quarter-century that separated the two
moments was a whirlwind of incessant and occasionally manic
activity in which Romero took on a steadily growing mountain of
pastoral and administrative responsibility, often driving himself to
the point of utter exhaustion and collapse.

One of his sacristans later testified to Romero's pace. "He was
on the go at all hours of the day and night. He never wasted an
opportunity!" At the end of one of his long days, after hearing
the confession of a parishioner, Romero mumbled a surprising
penance: "You should pray five pesos." "He had fallen asleep!"
laughed the sacristan when he told the story. "That's the way he
was. He would work without stopping until he was totally burned
out."[2]

Back in El Salvador, Romero was initially assigned to a small
mountain village called Anamorós, located not far from Ciudad
Barrios. His parish was forty-two square miles in size, most of
it accessible only by horseback. Romero was joined there by his
fourteen-year-old brother, Gaspar, who gladly took care of the

practicalities of everyday life, like cooking and fetching water from a nearby river.

Bishop Machado sent Romero to Anamorós for some hands-on pastoral experience, but just three months later called him to San Miguel to serve as his secretary. The entire diocese contained half a million Catholics but only twenty-one priests, which meant that each of them was the spiritual shepherd of some twenty-six thousand souls. Given his pressing need for clergy, Machado had no intention of letting one of his Rome-educated priests languish in a backwater. So Romero found himself living again in San Miguel, the city where he had attended minor seminary as a teenager. Once there, he was reunited with his old friend Valladares, who at an extraordinarily young age had been appointed Machado's vicar-general.

Serving as secretary to a diocesan bishop was as unglamorous a job as it sounds. Romero's tasks included tedious administrative work involved in overseeing the diocese's parishes, answering and filing correspondence, and in general making himself available for whatever task the bishop required of him.

And those tasks were never-ending because Bishop Machado didn't take his episcopal duties terribly seriously. According to Gaspar Romero, "He didn't leave the bishop's palace except to go to and from Mass. He didn't mix with people, he didn't participate in church activities, he didn't work, he had no plans, he didn't do a thing."[3] There were dark rumors that the bishop's real focus of attention was money-lending.

Given that Bishop Machado was uninterested in a hands-on approach when it came to running his diocese, most of the day-to-day work fell to Romero and Valladares—including, in Romero's case, eventually administering the diocesan minor seminary and serving as editor of the diocesan newspaper. Given his acute sense of duty, he must've found Machado's laziness a continuous source of exasperation on the one hand and an exciting opportunity for active ministry on the other. Because he and Valladares generally excelled at the assignments piled on them, not too many years passed before they were the two most powerful clerics in the diocese. After Valladares left San Miguel in 1956 to become an auxiliary bishop of San Salvador, even more responsibility fell on Romero's shoulders.

When Romero was appointed archbishop of San Salvador in 1977, there was some grumbling among the nation's priests that throughout his career he'd been a bureaucratic paper-pusher who had no real pastoral experience. Although it's true that Romero's administrative duties grew heavier as the years progressed, it's not the case that he lacked pastoral contact with the people. Despite being swamped by administrative duties for a few years in the late 1960s and early 1970s, he performed as a priest and not simply an administrator throughout his tenure at San Miguel. Bishop Machado appointed him pastor of the city's cathedral parish with additional responsibilities in two other smaller churches. Moreover, because he was secretary to the bishop, his pastoral mandate extended far beyond the parishes actually assigned to him.

In fact, the range and quantity of pastoral activities he took on are breathtaking. As well as celebrating Mass at least once a day, hearing confessions, leading rosary devotions, and tending to the individual spiritual needs of parishioners, Romero organized catechism classes throughout the diocese and was spiritual counselor to several young adult organizations. He served as chaplain to religious groups such as Catholic Action, the Franciscan

Third Order, the Knights of the Holy Sepulcher, Cursillo, and the Legion of Mary. He also developed a vibrant radio ministry. His preaching style caught on, and before long his sermons were so admired that they were broadcast each Sunday on practically all of San Miguel's radio stations.

Romero was especially devoted to Our Lady of Peace, San Miguel's patroness, whose statue was in San Francisco, one of the smaller churches in his charge. He carefully organized and joyfully participated in the annual November festivities held in her honor.

Even today, when religious fervor isn't as intense in El Salvador as it was in Romero's day, many *Migueleños* revere Our Lady of Peace. Her statue washed up on El Salvador's coastline in the seventeenth century, most likely flotsam from the shipwreck of a Spanish galleon. The people who discovered it carried the statue to San Miguel, whose residents were involved in a longstanding and bloody internecine feud. The story goes that upon seeing the statue, they fell to their knees and immediately renounced the violence that had ripped the city apart and spilled so much blood.

Remembering his own childhood in Ciudad Barrios as well as the poverty that befell his family in the final months of his father's life and after his death, Romero the pastor was especially mindful during his years in San Miguel of the poor and socially marginalized.

He organized the city's often homeless shoeshine boys into an association of mutual support and made sure that they were fed and had a place to sleep during the night other than the streets and doorways. He helped found a trade school to teach kids from poor families practical vocations. He was often seen at local jails and prisons, offering one-on-one counseling as well as weekly Masses to the prisoners, and occasionally even bringing films for them to watch. (He had come a long way from his youthful disdain for motion pictures.) He rounded up volunteer dietitians to teach people about proper nutrition. He gave away so many alms to beggars, prostitutes, and *campesinos* that he regularly depleted parish cash reserves. And he was particularly concerned to help people suffering from alcoholism, the disease from which both his father and his brother Gustavo suffered. "He was," said someone who knew him in those days, "like St. Vincent de Paul—a mass of poor people always followed him around."[4]

Romero also ministered to and was on friendly terms with San Miguel's wealthy *cafetaleros*. There was something about hobnobbing with them that undoubtedly thrilled the man who grew up on the wrong side of the tracks, and his longstanding companionship with sophisticated and blue-blooded Valladares gave him an entrée into their world. But more importantly, Romero believed until the day he died that the Gospel was intended for everyone, rich and poor alike, and he insisted that his duty as a priest was to minister to all social classes. He also recognized from a practical perspective that he needed the good will and generosity of the rich to maintain his ministry to the poor.

At the same time, Romero looked for no personal enrichment from them. He lived very simply, for many years using one of the spartan cells in a local convent as his private residence. At one point, some coffee-growers' wives decided that they'd surprise him by installing a new bed, curtains, and linens in his room. When Romero discovered what they'd done, he lost his temper and gave all the new things away. "I may be their friend," he sputtered, "but they're not going to start manipulating me, no matter how much money they have!"[5]

More than one of Romero's acquaintances experienced his short fuse during these years. Even his easy-going friend Valladares bore the brunt of it at times, although he characteristically made light of it. "This guy stresses himself out by getting so upset," he once said of Romero. "He blows his top so easily he's going to spend his entire life suffering from one sickness or another."[6]

Valladares was more correct than he could have known. Romero constantly struggled with stress that, until at least his final three years, was largely self-imposed. Partly because of his humble background, he felt the need to prove himself to others, and perhaps to God as well. Whatever the reasons, he was a perfectionist who demanded too much of himself. Not only did he stretch himself to the breaking point in taking on pastoral and administrative duties, but he also insisted on a punishing regimen of self-examination that bordered on what traditionally is known as "scrupulosity," a largely guilt-based sense of spiritual and moral inadequacy. Given this, his close lifelong relationship with Opus Dei, an ultra-conservative Catholic confraternity that stresses spiritual and bodily mortification as essential disciplines in the pursuit of holiness, it is perfectly understandable.

Romero's perfectionism exhausted him both physically and psychologically. His penance of "five pesos" is but one example of when he had squandered his stamina. In 1955, Bishop Machado, despite his heavy reliance on Romero, recognized that his secretary was killing himself with overwork and ordered him to take a three-month sabbatical.

At more than one period in his working life, Romero's chronic stress led him to unfounded worries about his mental stability. Once, during a time of particular anxiety and discouragement, he plaintively asked a fellow priest to assess his sanity. He also consulted a psychiatrist who concluded that Romero was perfectly sane but diagnosed him as obsessive-compulsive and suggested that he work on ameliorating his drive for perfection. Characteristically, however, Romero's efforts to break himself of it were more symptomatic than anodyne. He threw himself into even more intense devotions, retreats, and examinations of conscience, thereby only fueling his disorder.

Like many perfectionists, Romero's insecurity about what he perceived to be his own weaknesses sometimes provoked him to harsh and unfair criticisms of perceived weaknesses in his fellow priests. One particular bugaboo with him was sartorial propriety. He was ferociously hard on priests who, unlike himself, didn't wear cassocks—or, even worse, occasionally let themselves be seen in public in mufti. More substantively—and this is one of the ways in which his *romanità* revealed itself—he criticized what he considered to be the un-Vatican-like laxity of morals and flaccidity of spirit displayed by easygoing clerics in his diocese.

Unsurprisingly, Romero wasn't a favorite with all or even most of his fellow priests. They thought him too authoritarian, too coldly unimaginative, a regular company man and stickler for the rules. Also not surprisingly, many of them were envious of the power that Bishop Machado had given him. On at least one occasion, some of them unsuccessfully petitioned Machado to clip his secretary's wings.

But San Miguel's priests weren't the only ones who disliked what they considered to be Romero's heavy hand. When he ventured at times to criticize—always mildly—the government and the wealthy elite for their treatment of the *campesinos,* they accused him of being a Communist, an accusation that was dangerously incendiary ever since the *la Matanza* revolt of 1932. Yet when he urged the *campesinos* to trust in God and resist violent responses to the injustice they suffered, he was accused by left-leaning union organizers of being little more than a shill for the nation's powermongers.

One of those organizers, Maria Varona, was especially critical of what she took to be Romero's wishy-washiness. "Do you want me to be frank?" she recalled in an interview after his death. "Father Romero? He was a friend of the poor and a friend of the rich.... He went around with sheep and with wolves, and his thinking was that the sheep and the wolves should eat from the same dish, because that's what was pleasing to God."[7] As far as Varona was concerned, eating from the same dish as wolves meant that eventually the sheep would become part of the meal.

Romero was also on bad terms with San Miguel's Protestants and Masons. Like so many pre–Vatican II Roman Catholics, he considered the former apostates—separated sisters and brothers who, he prayed, would come to their senses and retract their errors—and the latter outright heathens. Both were gustily and regularly denounced in his sermons, talks, and newspaper articles. He also disallowed Christian burial for Masons and even refused permission for a ceremony honoring Gerardo Barrios— the past Salvadoran president after whom Romero's own hometown was named—to be held in the cathedral because Barrios had been a Mason. After he became archbishop, Romero's attitude to Protestants thankfully became more ecumenical and even friendly. Not so, however, with Masons.

To his great credit, Romero was uncomfortably aware of how demanding and judgmental he could be with others, and he considered it a grave fault. In the mid-1950s, he went on the full thirty-day Ignatian retreat in which a Jesuit director led him through

St. Ignatius Loyola's sixteenth-century Spiritual Exercises. One of their purposes is to help participants discern spiritual, moral, and psychological tendencies in themselves that may stand in the way of a richer relationship with God and their sisters and brothers. The retreat's opportunity for sustained self-examination apparently planted seeds of fruitful contrition in Romero that gradually yielded richer and richer harvests of generosity and tolerance. But it would take a few more years.

The 1960s saw two Church councils that profoundly influenced Romero's view of the world, Roman Catholicism, and himself. The first was Vatican II, which met in his beloved city of Rome from 1962 to 1965. The second was the 1968 gathering of Latin American bishops in Medellín, Colombia. As a loyal son of the Church, Romero for the most part was a defender of Vatican II reforms, even though his approval at times may have been directed more at the council's abstract principles than the concrete actions they inspired in some of his younger colleagues. But as we'll see in the next chapter, the views on how the Church should respond to the economic and political situation in Latin American that came out of Medellín gave rise to a real spiritual crisis for Romero that took him several years to resolve.

In October 1958, following the death of Pius XII, Angelo Roncalli, Patriarch of Venice, was elected pope and took the name John XXIII. Already in his late seventies, the new pope was intended by the College of Cardinals to be a do-nothing placeholder who would allow the Vatican ship of state to continue on its steady course. But John had different ideas. He soon stunned the curia by announcing that he intended to convene the ecumenical gathering that became known as the Vatican II Council.

The immediately prior major Church councils, Trent in the mid-sixteenth century and Vatican I in 1870, had been largely reactive in nature, called by popes who felt beleaguered, by Protestantism in the case of Trent and modernity in the case of Vatican I. In both, what resulted were decisions that served only to further alienate the Church from non-Catholic culture. The attending bishops hoped that their decisions would insulate the Church from external threats. But they only made the world look more hostile to the faithful and more threatening to Catholic identity, which in turn made the Church hierarchy more fixated than ever on circling the wagons.

John XXIII didn't want his council to repeat this mistake. Concerned that the Church had become a self-enclosed and dusty museum, he intended to throw open its windows so that fresh air could blow away the staleness. Having served as a Vatican diplomat to several nations for most of his career, he had a broad perspective and deep appreciation of secular as well as interfaith culture. He realized that the Church could profit from reaching out to the world, just as the world could be enriched by the message the Church proclaimed.

It took a while to prepare for the council, but the first of four sessions finally opened in October 1962, four years after John became pope. Some 2,500 bishops from around the world descended on Rome, accompanied by an army of *periti,* theological advisors who were some of the Church's finest thinkers. (In 2005, one of them, Joseph Ratzinger, became Pope Benedict XVI.) John, already showing signs of the stomach cancer that would kill him less than a year later, opened that initial session with a profoundly hopeful message. "The human family," he said, "is on the threshold of a new era," and the Church is called to cross that threshold with the rest of humanity. Referring to himself in the royal "we" as was the custom of popes in those days, John chided conservative prelates of the Church who tried to slam shut the door on that threshold.

> It sometimes happens that We hear certain opinions which disturb Us—opinions expressed by people who, though fired with a commendable zeal for religion, are lacking in sufficient prudence and judgment in their evaluation of events. They can see nothing but calamity and disaster in the present state of the world. They say over and over that this modern age of ours, in comparison with past ages, is definitely deteriorating. One would think from their attitude that history, that great teacher of life, had taught them nothing. They seem to imagine that in the days of the earlier councils everything was as it should be so far as doctrine and morality and the Church's rightful liberty were concerned.
>
> We feel that We must disagree with these prophets of doom, who are always forecasting worse disasters, as though the end of the world were at hand.[8]

John died in June 1963. His successor, Paul VI, steered the remaining three sessions of Vatican II in the direction that John had intended. By the time the Council adjourned for the final time in December 1965, the attending bishops had approved sixteen documents on topics that included doctrinal clarification, Scripture, revelation, tradition, worship and liturgy, and Christian engagement in the world.

Pope John envisioned a revitalization of the Church, and the reforms instigated by Vatican II aimed at precisely that. Changes in liturgy included celebrating in the vernacular with the priest facing the assembly and the people playing a more active role. Study of Scripture by the laity was strongly encouraged; no longer would the Bible be the near-exclusive preserve of clergy and scholars. A spirit of ecumenical dialogue among the various Christian traditions was also encouraged, and initial steps in building interfaith relations were taken, particularly when it came to the other two religions, Judaism and Islam, that shared Christianity's Abrahamic roots. This was a check on the imperial Church's claim that she was absolutely superior to other Christian traditions as well as other faiths. Finally, the Church's social teachings, pretty well established at least since the 1891 promulgation of Leo XIII's encyclical *Rerum Novarum*, were soundly reaffirmed, as was the Church's evangelical mission to bring the message of Christ, the Light of the World, to all peoples and nations.

Given the thin-skinned intolerance for which Romero became known and disliked in the late 1960s and early 1970s, some commentators have concluded that the reforms of Vatican II must have disconcerted and even alarmed him. But the truth of the matter is that he seemed to be largely sympathetic with what the Council was doing. He closely studied the documents as they were released, returning to them again and again, approvingly concluding that "the return to the Gospel was the characteristic, insistent note of Vatican II."[9]

However, Romero also feared that many Salvadoran Catholics might be upset by the Council, feeling that its reforms, especially the liturgical changes, had pulled the rug out from under their feet. So in his sermons and radio addresses he reassured them that they had nothing to fear. Sounding remarkably like John XXIII, he insisted that the Church is perennially called to respond to historical change, and that local traditions, however comfortable they may feel, ought never to be confused with essential doctrine. The latter remains solidly permanent, the former peripheral and fungible. The spiritual and moral clarification that Romero saw arising from the Council was, he was confident, the work of the Holy Spirit. He came to admire Paul VI, who made sure that John's dream of throwing open the Church's windows was fulfilled, almost as much as he did Pius XI.

What Romero did take exception to, however, was what he saw as the way some priests treated the reforms of Vatican II as licenses to step outside the boundaries defined by the Church, especially when it came to the liturgy. Even worse, he thought, was using Vatican II as a pretext for conflating political agitation with the tenets of faith. Romero was more or less comfortable with reform, but not with corrupting the Good News by equating it with politics or, especially, revolution. He would continue to refine his views on the proper relationship between faith and politics over the next few years. But he never wavered in his insistence that the Church's mission was conversion of hearts and minds, not power politics.

Romero's prominence and years of service in San Miguel led many people, including himself, to just assume he was the obvious choice to succeed Bishop Machado. As things turned out, though, he'd made too many enemies. He was skipped over, quite possibly on Machado's own recommendation, by the Vatican's appointment of Lawrence Graziano as San Miguel's coadjutor bishop in 1965. Bishop coadjutors nearly always succeed the sitting bishop. They are appointed to get some on-the-job training before they take over the see. Predictably, Graziano became bishop of San Miguel when Machado finally retired in January 1968.

There's little doubt that Romero was hurt and humiliated by Graziano's appointment. Not only was the new bishop not even a Salvadoran—he was born in the Bronx—but he was also younger and had a narrower range of professional experience than Romero. True, he'd been auxiliary bishop in another diocese for a number of years and so already had executive experience. But given the responsibilities loaded on him by Machado, so did Romero, even though he had performed them without episcopal rank.

It was probably inevitable that the two men would clash. Romero couldn't help but feel resentful and, given his scrupulosity, guilty for doing do, which made him even testier. Graziano, less willing to delegate as freely as Machado had, pulled back some of Romero's duties—which of course Romero took as a personal slight. Moreover, Graziano was less formal in both style and appearance than the perfectionist Romero demanded from a prelate of the Church. So the tension between them became palpable, erupting on at least one occasion when Graziano actually dressed down Romero in public. It quickly became clear that there wasn't enough room in the diocese for them both.

So, a measure was taken not uncommon in institutional structures: a "troublemaker" is given a titular promotion and moved out, thereby getting rid of him while allowing him to save face. On April 4, 1967, in honor of his silver anniversary as a priest, Romero was named a monseñor, or monsignor. Just a few months later he was appointed secretary of the Episcopal Conference of El Salvador (CEDES). Happily for Graziano, the new position required Romero's relocation to San Salvador, the capital city where he'd spent six months as a youth before traveling to Rome for seminary studies. Romero departed San Miguel on September 1. He had just turned fifty and was about to begin the most miserable seven years of his life.

Many *Migueleños* were distressed at his departure, especially those who had rooted for him to be their new bishop, and in their disappointment, some of them even accused Bishop Graziano of exiling him. Graziano promptly smoothed things over by publicly praising Romero, who in turn publicly thanked him. But others, like Maria Varona who criticized Romero for playing both sides of the field, couldn't have cared less. When he left, she sourly recalled, "everyone applauded and burst into tears because after twenty-three years he was leaving San Miguel. But as for me personally, I can't say that I was too sorry to see him go."[10]

CHAPTER FOUR

Dark Years

"He [was] the pastor to his paperwork."[1]

The short fuse that Romero displayed only occasionally in San Miguel seemed perpetually lit during the seven years he spent in San Salvador as an administrator and auxiliary bishop. He was constantly unhappy, insecure, defensive, and angry, and at odds with his fellow priests, the archbishop of San Salvador, and proponents of the way of understanding the Gospel that became known as liberation theology. This period, 1967–1974, was unquestionably the darkest of his personal life.

The cause for Romero's unhappiness during these years is complex. Despite the fact that he'd been made a monseñor and secretary of CEDES, his humiliating failure to succeed Bishop Machado, not to mention the eagerness with which Bishop Graziano whisked him out of San Miguel, must have continued to eat away at him.

Then there was his scrupulosity, that ever-present sense of inadequacy and unworthiness which burdened him throughout much of his life. Coupled with Romero's hurt pride during this bleak period was a guilty sense that such a response was unworthy in a servant of God.

Finally, Romero felt isolated during these years. He had never been particularly good at making friends. He was a caring pastor, and warmly loyal to the few close acquaintances he had. But he was essentially an introvert who found it difficult to adjust comfortably on a personal level to new faces and unfamiliar surroundings. As someone who knew him after his relocation to San Salvador recalled, "He was always hiding…Romero was a loner."[2]

Had he chosen to live by himself, Romero's standoffishness may not have been so terribly noticeable. But he moved into the dormitory of his old seminary, the Jesuit-run San José de la Montaña, most probably because it also headquartered CEDES and offered affordable room and board to a priest like Romero who lacked the financial resources for other accommodations. Living in such an environment demands a lot of interaction with others. But as one of the Jesuits remembered, Romero "started off on the wrong foot from the very beginning…. He was an insignificant being, a shadow that went by clinging to the walls…. He never ate any of his meals with us. He would go down to the dining room at different times so that he wouldn't run into us."

The upshot? "I didn't like him." Neither, apparently, did most of the other Jesuits at the seminary.[3]

In all fairness, Romero was too busy for a lot of socializing, even if he had wanted to. As CEDES secretary, his immediate responsibility was synthesizing and summarizing a mountain of documents to prepare El Salvador's bishops for a conference planned the following year in Medellín, Columbia. His fellow dormitory residents often heard him clacking away at his portable typewriter late into the night.

The Medellín Conference, which would wrap up its work almost exactly a year after Romero's move to San Salvador, proved to be a watershed for the Latin American Church. Called to discern the best ways to apply the social teachings of Vatican II in the specific economic and political contexts of Latin America, the conference was opened by Pope Paul VI, the first pontiff to visit that part of the world. While there, the pope proclaimed that the Church's mission is "to personify the Christ of a poor and hungry people," and admonished the wealthy "to detach from the stability of your position...of privilege in order to serve those who need your wealth."[4] In saying this, Paul was reiterating what the Vatican II document *Gaudium et Spes* had stated in its opening sentence: Disciples of Christ are called to be especially mindful of the poor and the afflicted.

The Latin American bishops who attended the conference basically put liberation theology on Catholicism's map, and they did so with the support of Pope Paul. Recognizing that the fundamental material and spiritual problem in Latin America was the enormous imbalance of wealth and power, and insisting that they "cannot remain indifferent in the face of the tremendous social injustice...which keep[s] the majority of our peoples in dismal poverty," the bishops maintained that laws and social institutions which preserved the status quo were sinful; that the teaching of Jesus obliged the Church to exercise a "preferential option" for the vulnerable poor who in many cases suffer from "inhuman wretchedness"; that the Church is charged with grassroots evangelization to help the poor become more aware of their situation, to see how their treatment by the rich and powerful conflicts with the teachings of the Gospel, and to empower them to work for their liberation; and that occasional charity neither can nor should substitute for systematic justice.[5]

To put legs on these principles, the bishops at Medellín also recommended the creation of basic Christian communities (usually referred to as "base" communities) that would gather together a close-knit group of *campesinos,* train them in reading and expounding the Gospel to their fellows as "delegates of the Word," and encourage them to organize clinics, schools, and cooperatives. In doing so, the bishops invited a reconsideration of the top-down hierarchical flow that was the norm in Roman Catholic ministry and polity.[6]

The Jesuits at San José de la Montaña were enthusiastic about the Medellín recommendations and immediately began to teach and put them into practice. For his part, Romero worried that the conference's conclusions went too far and risked destabilizing the Church. His greatest fear was that they conflated a political agenda with Christian mission, thereby bestowing a misguided imprimatur upon the class warfare favored by Marxists. In fact, he suspected that a good deal of liberation theology was inspired by or even the pawn of Communist propagandists, despite the Medellín bishops' denunciation of both capitalist and Communist excesses. One of his acquaintances at the time recalled that Romero's face would go taut and his lower lip twitch at the mere mention of Medellín.

Romero's own position was that a genuine liberation theology should strive first and foremost for the liberation or salvation of individual souls from sin, and only then address issues of inequality and injustice. What he wanted was what he called the *salvación integral* of human beings that focused on both spiritual conversion and material well-being. This, he insisted, was genuine liberation theology, and radical priests who, seized by "a psychosis of rancorous prophetism," allowed themselves to be carried away by enthusiasm for political agitation betrayed it.[7]

Part of Romero's uneasiness with Medellín undoubtedly was

rooted in his *romanità* fidelity to tradition as defined by the conservative Vatican curia. For the greater part of his adult life, his understanding of the priestly role centered on liturgy, devotions, and sacraments. The priest's unique calling was to minister to the spiritual needs of his parishioners, not to meddle in their material lives or get involved in politics.

Relations between Romero and the Jesuits at San José were bad enough before Medellín. Afterward, however, they became horrible, with Romero feeling himself surrounded by enemies and the Jesuits in turn doing little to disguise their disdain for the strange interloper who lived in their seminary. Thus began the feud between Romero and El Salvador's Jesuits that continued until the late 1970s, notwithstanding the fact that Romero had been trained by Jesuits and was a devotee of the Ignatian spiritual exercises.

In the midst of Romero's war of words and ideas with proponents of liberation theology, an actual, though mercifully brief, shooting war broke out between El Salvador and Honduras. Frequently called the "Soccer War" because it was immediately preceded by a bitter sports rivalry between the two nations, its real cause was the Honduran government's forced deportation of over a hundred thousand Salvadorans back to their native land. Having left El Salvador for Honduras in search of work, they were sent back to an economy where 20 percent of adults were unemployed and 40 percent underemployed. Their return to an already financially struggling nation created a flashpoint of tension between Honduras and El Salvador.

The Soccer War of July 1969 ended in five days. But the Salvadoran economic crisis, with its escalating unemployment, low wages, and increased concentration of wealth in a few elite families, continued. In just a few years, the poverty and violence that it wrought would become the focus of Romero's ministry.

In mid-1968, Romero was appointed Executive Secretary of the Episcopal Secretariat of Central America and Panama (SEDAC), a position that required him to travel frequently to Guatemala, where SEDAC was headquartered. Several months into the job, the bishop members of the conference decided that their executive secretary should be a fellow bishop. Since none of them wished to take on the responsibility, San Salvador Archbishop Luis Chávez y González was prevailed on to request that the pope name Romero an auxiliary bishop, even though Chavez already had a perfectly competent auxiliary bishop in Arturo Rivera y Damas. The archbishop wasn't crazy about the idea. Although he respected Romero's pastoral dedication, Chávez disagreed with his negative appraisal of Medellín's endorsement of liberation theology.

Nevertheless, Romero received a notification from the papal nuncio in April 1970 that he had been appointed bishop. He was given one day to accept or decline. Romero the perfectionist felt rushed, and afterward would second-guess his motives for accepting the appointment, just as years earlier he questioned his motives prior to his priestly ordination. But accept he did, and the consecration took place two months later. Romero took as his episcopal motto a line from the Ignatian Exercises: *Sentir con la Iglesia*—"To Be of One Mind and Heart with the Church." What the motto signified for Romero then would take on a different inflection in just a few years. In 1970, he understood *la Iglesia* primarily as an ecclesial institution. By the end of his life, it came to mean for him the People of God.

Fr. Rutilio Grande García, the only Jesuit at the San José seminary with whom Romero had made friends, served as master of ceremonies for the event. It came across as a lavish affair, with wealthy dignitaries, including the president of El Salvador, attending. Given the nation's economic situation, Romero was criticized for what many considered to be his tone-deafness. Already disliked and distrusted by most of his fellow priests, the ceremony only strengthened their conviction that Romero was in the pockets of the nation's moneyed and political elite and out of touch with the nation's poor. There was some measure of truth to the claim.

The feud between Bishop Romero and practically every one of his clerical colleagues began almost immediately. Following on the heels of his consecration was an earlier scheduled pastoral week in which Archbishop Chávez met with the nation's priests to discuss how to apply Medellín's social justice principles locally. Romero attended only one or two sessions, keeping in the background and refusing to participate in the conversation. But a couple of weeks later he published an article in the diocesan newspaper *Orientación* blasting a couple of Jesuits who, he charged, had preached Marxist ideology at the meeting instead of the Gospel. The paper later published a furious rejoinder by the Jesuits he had attacked. But Romero didn't back down one bit.

Realizing Romero had a flair for journalism, Chávez eventually appointed him editor of *Orientación*. Throughout his three years at the paper's helm he used his position to inveigh against liberal priests in general and Jesuits in particular. Under his direction, the paper took a sharp turn to the right, focusing on traditional moral issues, such as alcoholism and drug abuse, avoiding thorny criticisms of high-level governmental and oligarchical corruption, and even defending what was basically a coup d'etat that pre-empted the 1972 presidential election results.

After decades of rule by military strongmen, El Salvador finally had its first legitimate election in 1967. Hope was high among the nation's liberals and progressives that the nation had segued from strongman rule to democracy. But the Soccer War deflated this hope by creating a wave of patriotic nationalism, and in 1972 the military rode it to regain political control of the country. Although José Napoleón Duarte Fuentes, the presidential candidate of a coalition of Christian Democrats, Social Democrats, and moderate socialists that went by the acronym UNO won the election, the military, spuriously charging voter fraud, refused to let him take office. When public protests erupted, a state of national emergency was declared and the military's candidate, Colonel Arturo Armando Molina, whom Romero considered a personal friend, was declared president. Repression of dissent followed swiftly and harshly as Molina cracked down on his critics. Shamefully, CEDES, the conference of El Salvador bishops, made no objection to Molina's seizure of power or the subsequent arrest and exile of Duarte. By the time elections were held again two years later, the military stranglehold on the nation was so firm that the government simply declared all of the ruling party's candidates de facto winners.

One of Molina's first victims was the University of El Salvador, which had a reputation for liberalism. Nearly one thousand instructors and students were beaten and arrested, the university president banished from the country, and classes suspended for an entire year. CEDES, of which Romero was still secretary, once again refused to buck the authorities by denouncing the outrage. As one disgusted Salvadoran priest recalled, "The Bishops' Conference published a paid ad in the newspapers, written and signed by Monseñor Romero as secretary, defending the occupation of the university with a rationalization taken straight from the government's statement: that the university was a hotbed of subversion and that it was necessary to take measures against it."[8]

Shortly after Molina shut down the university, Romero was invited to celebrate Mass at the parish of Zacamil, where several thriving base communities had taken root. He accepted, but was clearly wary of what awaited him. He was right to be, because the priests and laypersons gathered there immediately challenged his support of the government. Romero responded defensively and in a high-handed tone. "I want to tell you," he scolded, "that I don't agree with the one-sided way in which you have been using your faith!" Accusations and counteraccusations flew back and forth until Romero shouted, "You're not doing pastoral work here at all. You're doing political work! And you haven't called me to a Mass. You've called me to a meeting of subversives!"

That was the final straw. One of the priests who'd invited Romero announced that "in this environment of distrust, even though we're all part of the same Church, we don't have the conditions necessary to be able to celebrate Mass.... So let's just call it off. The Mass is over!"[9] Romero left, furious. The episode only underscored his distrust of the base communities movement.

That distrust was more than shared by the authorities. Terror tactics against *campesinos* who were viewed as subversives—especially those who were involved in base communities as delegates of the Word—stepped up following Molina's ascension to power. People were snatched from their villages, homes, and fields; their bodies, often found mutilated, were discovered a couple days later in public places.

But Romero, while personally deploring the violence, remained publicly focused on guarding what he considered to be the purity of the Church's mission. His next major shot across the bow in defense of *la Iglesia* was in May 1973.

It came in an *Orientación* editorial he wrote entitled "Liberating Education, but Christian and without Demagoguery." In it, Romero attacked San Salvador's Jesuit-run school, Externado San José, for teaching what he considered to be subversion to its students. He claimed that the teachers were drilling young minds in Marxist indoctrination while ignoring or distorting the traditional teachings of the Church. Although he acknowledged that education in Latin America was badly in need of a curricular overhauling, he insisted that Jesuitical demagoguery wasn't the way to go about it.

His editorial stirred up a hornets' nest, especially since many of the students at the Externado were from some of San Salvador's well-heeled and ruling families. Secular newspapers throughout the city picked up the topic, misreporting Romero's opinion as the official position of the Church.

Fr. Francisco Estrada, the Jesuit provincial, was incensed by Romero's attack. "He said that our Marxist teachings pitted children against their parents. He said we were using 'pamphlets of Communist origin' in our religion classes. Outrageous accusations!"

When Estrada personally confronted Romero, demanding that the bishop back up his charges with hard evidence, Romero demurred. "I want to know what you are basing these accusations on!" shouted Estrada. But Romero "kept his eyes downcast and responded simply: 'I have reliable sources of information.'" He refused to say anything more, leaving Estrada convinced that the bishop either had no sources or that he knew the ones he had were dubious.[10]

The uproar over Romero's editorial got so out of hand that Archbishop Chávez, already irked by his auxiliary bishop's intransigent belligerence toward the Jesuits, stepped in. He put together an investigatory team of priests to examine the school's curriculum. They not only found no evidence of Marxist indoctrination; they also discovered that the vast percentage of student parents fully backed the instruction being offered. Chávez instructed Romero to publish these conclusions in *Orientación*. He did so, but rather petulantly buried them on the paper's last page and editorialized that the findings were questionable. This was, however, defensive bravado. A man as insecure as Romero must've been humiliated by yet another public dressing-down from an ecclesial superior.

Curiously, Romero seems to have been clueless about how much damage his criticism of the Jesuits was doing to the credibility of the Salvadoran Church and the safety of its priests. He sincerely believed he was upholding the one and doing no harm to the other. But *Orientación*'s continuous accusation that at least some clerics had been infected by Marxism and were trying to subvert the established order through political agitation only provided ammunition for the persecution of priests. As early as 1970, the year Romero was named auxiliary bishop, Fr. Nicolas Rodriguez, who ministered to *campesinos* in northern El Salvador, had been assassinated by national guardsmen. Archbishop Chávez sent his newest bishop to transport the corpse to San Salvador. Yet the lesson that Romero might have learned from this shocking murder didn't sink in.

Following closely on the failed campaign against the Externado was another embarrassing setback for Romero that again involved the Jesuits, even if only tangentially this time.

Since 1915, the Society of Jesus had operated the major seminary of San José de la Montaña, the same one that Romero had briefly attended and in whose dormitory he lived for a while when he left San Miguel for San Salvador. Over the years, it had trained most of the diocesan priests who served throughout El Salvador.

By 1970, the Jesuits' enthusiasm for Medellín was a thorn in the side of most of the Salvadoran bishops, including Romero. For their part, the Jesuits, increasingly stretched by their educational commitments at the Central American University they had established in 1965, were looking to downsize their presence at San José. So it was decided that the leadership of the seminary would transfer from the Jesuits to the bishops.

The Jesuits recommended one of their own, Romero's friend Rutilio Grande, to serve as the transition rector. Grande had been teaching at the seminary and was well qualified to be its leader. But a fiery homily he'd given on the Feast of the Transfiguration criticizing the nation's wealthy Catholics for "put[ting] a dam of selfishness in front of the message of Jesus our Savior" infuriated all the bishops except Chávez and Rivera, and they rejected his nomination.[11] Instead, they offered the rectorship to Romero. He in turn declined in favor of a priest who, to the dismay of the bishops, left the seminary's liberal policy and code of conduct they found so objectionable relatively untouched. So two years later, the Salvadoran bishops sent the Jesuits packing once and for all, and replaced the offending rector with Romero, who this time accepted the position.

It was a disaster from the very start. The priest whom Romero appointed as vice rector and who was responsible for the day-to-day business of the seminary proved to be an overly harsh disciplinarian heartily despised by faculty and students alike. Most of the theology and philosophy instruction was relocated to other schools, and the curriculum was reduced to a handful of what today would be called remedial courses. Since both program and enrollment in the seminary were insignificant compared to what they'd been under the Jesuits, the whole enterprise began to lose the trust of the bishops, who soon ceased sending seminarians from their dioceses. It quickly became apparent that there wasn't enough revenue coming in to maintain the seminary buildings and grounds, and by mid-1971, the entire enterprise collapsed. The bishops, eager to cut their losses, voted to close down San José.

A fellow bishop recalled that Romero was downcast and chagrined at his failure to keep the seminary afloat. Given his perfectionism, his reaction is understandable. In all fairness to him, however, the project was doomed. The Salvadoran bishops simply weren't committed to supporting the seminary with either students or funds. One suspects that for at least some of them, ousting the Jesuits was their first priority, taking over and actually running San José a distant second. Nevertheless, Romero took the debacle as a black mark on his administrative abilities. It was yet another public humiliation.

A third blow was to come. It fell shortly after the seminary project fizzled out and, predictably, it came from the Jesuits. The Central American University published in its magazine *Estudios Centroamericanos (ECA)* a damning indictment of *Orientación* under Romero's editorship. It concluded that the newspaper favored the political and economic status quo and resisted criticisms of the nation's political and oligarchical strongmen. Moreover, the article claimed that "the paper criticizes injustice in the abstract but criticizes methods of liberation in the concrete."[12] Interpreted in the most benign way possible, the authors of the report accused editor Romero of vacillation and willful ignorance. Interpreted truer to the authors' intentions, it charged him with hypocrisy and kowtowing to Salvador's power elite.

By this time Romero's relationship with Archbishop Chávez, as well as that with fellow San Salvador Auxiliary Bishop Rivera, had deteriorated almost to the breaking point. Chávez and Rivera were the only two prelates in the nation's conference of bishops who supported, even if with some reservations, the recommendations of Medellín. Romero was already disgruntled with the archbishop because he had refused to back him in the Esternado debate. Now, with the publication of *ECA*'s report, Romero took it into his head that Rivera had somehow engineered it. Rivera denied any complicity, but Romero didn't believe him.

Romero's final editorial for *Orientación* was written in October 1974. He came out swinging, defiant to the last, blasting those who used the language of religion

> to destroy the basis of religion. In the name of faith, those who have lost their faith have tried to struggle against the faith. And this is very sad, truly sad. For our part, we have preferred to adhere to that which is certain, to cling with fear and trembling to the Rock of Peter...instead of leaping like reckless and foolhardy acrobats to the speculations of the impudent thinkers of social movements of dubious origin.[13]

Some of Romero's anger at the *ECA* denunciation was justifiable. It is true that both personally and professionally he had been worried about what he saw as the eagerness with which too many clerics and laypersons subordinated their faith to politics and insisted that doing so was a distortion of both Vatican II and Medellín. It is also the case that he was slow to speak out against some of the more egregious abuses perpetrated by the nation's elite—including the hijacking of the 1972 and 1974 elections.

But under Romero's editorship, *Orientación* did push for the rights of *campesinos* to a living wage and better working conditions, and criticized their mistreatment by the landowners. In his own articles, Romero reminded readers that the *campesinos,* made just like the rich in the image of God and hence endowed with inherent dignity, were not pariahs. They had a right, he affirmed, to form labor unions and to negotiate for better wages and working conditions, and the wealthy landed class had the obligation to listen and respond to them. But that was about as far as he was prepared to go during his time as editor.

It took years for Romero's resentment of Bishop Rivera to cool down. It was still red hot in 1974 when the Salvadoran bishops elected him to represent them at a bishops' synod to be held in Rome that October. Romero declined, whereupon to his dismay the bishops selected Rivera to take his place. Romero quickly let it be known that he'd changed his mind and was willing to go to Rome after all. Unfortunately for him, the Vatican had already given Rivera his delegate credentials.

The overwhelming impression by friend and foe alike of Romero during these dark years is that he was a lonely, anxious, and angry man. The series of failed projects he attempted, the continuous burden of his fellow priests' dislike and distrust, and his own feelings of insecurity, unfulfillment, and guilt were at times unbearable.

His psychological distress took a toll on him physically. In addition to his usual aches and pains, Romero grew gravely ill in the autumn of 1970 with a respiratory complaint that seems to have turned into a bad case of bronchitis or pneumonia. He needed a couple months to recuperate, and when he was well enough, a concerned Chávez sent him off to Mexico for a much-needed rest. Romero wound up staying there four months, recovering his physical health and mental equilibrium.

During his respiratory illness, he was nursed by one of his few lay friends, Salvador Barraza, whom he met in 1959 when Barraza made a business trip to San Miguel. Barraza took the ailing bishop into his home and nursed him until he was well enough to head off to Mexico. Romero and the Barraza family grew very close during that time, and in later years the bishop went to them whenever he needed a break from the burdens of his office. Romero was comfortable enough in their domestic circle to shed his episcopal reserve. He'd settle himself into an easy chair, kick off his shoes, and watch television with the children. He felt at home with them.

As a small businessman, Barraza was fortunate enough to have more free time than many other Salvadorans, and he and Romero frequently journeyed on day trips to the seashore or vacationed in Mexico and Guatemala. Barraza also doubled as Romero's chauffeur whenever the auxiliary bishop made pastoral visits. Their relationship grew even closer after Romero was named archbishop of San Salvador in 1977. During the dark years, Romero's friendship with Barraza was one of the very few bright spots.

CHAPTER FIVE

First Stirrings

"The man wanted to learn."[1]

During the bishops' synod that Rivera attended in Romero's place, something happened which began to set the man distrusted and disliked by his fellow priests on a different path: Romero was named the new bishop of Santiago de María. He would shepherd it for the two years leading up to his 1977 appointment as archbishop of San Salvador. His time there would begin to stir in him the beginnings of an awareness that Medellín's analysis of the Church's mission was worthy of serious consideration.

Romero's new diocese was geographically expansive, stretching from the Pacific coast all the way to Honduras, and it included Romero's hometown of Ciudad Barrios. Much of it was situated at a high altitude, enabling Romero to enjoy a cooler climate than he had become accustomed to in San Salvador. The diocese contained two largish towns, but most of its half-million residents were *campesinos* who worked the huge coffee, cotton, and sugar cane plantations owned by a handful of families. Two-thirds of the diocese's population lived in poverty.

In fact, the diocese itself, notwithstanding the presence in it of a few wealthy landowners, was the poorest in El Salvador, a sad state of affairs recognized by even the Vatican. When Romero was informed of his appointment as its bishop, he flew to Rome to thank Pope Paul personally. The pope presented him with a chalice, a not unusual personal gift for a new bishop, but also gave a badly needed $5,000 contribution—or, more accurately, foreign aid—to Romero's new diocese.

Santiago de María was a relatively young diocese, carved just twenty years earlier out of the then unmanageably huge diocese of San Miguel. Romero was only its second bishop. The man he succeeded, Francisco José Castro y Ramírez, had distanced himself from his priests and people, much like the bishop Romero had worked for during his years in San Miguel. Romero determined that he would offer the diocese a different sort of leadership. He wanted to be the friend as well as the pastor of the twenty-five priests in his charge. He wanted to offer them, and himself, a fresh start.

Because of his tendency toward scrupulosity further intensified by the emphasis of the Ignatian Exercises and Opus Dei on self-examination, Romero had long been introspective, sometimes obsessively so. During his dark years in San Salvador, he had gone on several retreats that gave him the time and solitude to reflect on his personality quirks and how they affected his relationships with others. Given that he was perennially at odds with most of his fellow clerics during this period, such self-examination likely took on a special urgency for him.

During two of these retreats in 1971 and 1972, Romero came to the breakthrough realization that his self-demanding perfectionism as well as his rigidity with others were defense mechanisms spawned by insecurity that he believed originated in his childhood. He recognized that both these traits tended to make him stiff, unapproachable, and intolerant, and that his strategy for dealing with the relative friendlessness that consequently befell him was to throw himself into work—which, given his temperament, only exasperated the perfectionism and rigidity to which he was prone.[2]

Romero determined not to let his personal failings sour his new Santiago de María relationships as they had his San Salvador ones. So even before his formal episcopal installation in December 1974, he went out of his way to get acquainted with his priests and assure them that, unlike his predecessor, he intended to listen to them, seek their counsel, and welcome genuine collaboration with them. He even invited them to offer criticisms of his performance as bishop, a potential public humiliation he would have thought intolerable during his years as auxiliary bishop of San Salvador.

Romero also wanted to win the confidence of the people whom he would be shepherding. In many ways, this was easier than winning over suspiciously wary clerics, because Romero's greatest gifts were always pastoral. During his two decades as a priest in San Miguel, he had established good pastoral relations with both wealthy elites and *campesinos*, working tirelessly to carry out his priestly duties on their behalf. His appointment to Santiago de María gave him the opportunity to escape the bureaucratic paper pushing and administrative snake pits, which, for the most part, had extinguished any meaningful pastoral role for his seven long years in San Salvador. More than one observer noted that Romero seemed much happier, less anxious, and less intolerant in Santiago de María.

In many ways, his pastoral presence in his new diocese was a repeat of his conduct during his San Miguel days. He traveled constantly throughout its vast region. Given the extreme shortage of priests in both his diocese and the nation as a whole, many of his parishes, some with an astounding fifty thousand parishioners, had overwhelming unmet pastoral needs. Since the diocese was without a radio station powerful enough to transmit the new bishop's homilies and messages to all the towns and villages in his charge, Romero once again rigged vehicles up with loudspeakers so that he could preach as he traveled, pausing frequently in fields where *campesinos* labored to offer words of encouragement and celebrate the Eucharist. When the roads gave way to rough mountain trails inaccessible by vehicles, he proceeded on to the remoter corners of his diocese on mule or foot.

Some of the exuberance with which Romero embraced these pastoral visits can be discerned from the fact that he often frustrated his priests by failing to record baptisms and marriages. Romero the San Salvador administrator had been a meticulous stickler when it came to keeping records. He always insisted that things be done strictly by the book. Romero the pastoral bishop had other priorities.

The range of his pastoral activities also included making sure that lay-led associations such as Cursillo, Caritas, and support groups for recovering alcoholics got the diocesan support they needed. Additionally, drawing upon his journalistic experience, Romero launched a weekly diocesan periodical, *El Apóstol,* to which he regularly contributed a column called "The Pastor's Voice"—not, significantly, "The *Bishop's* Voice."

For all his intentions to turn over a leaf when it came to human relationships, the new spiritual leader of Santiago de María brought to his job the same dislike of Medellín-inspired activism that he had acquired in San Salvador. His personal timidity as well as his willingness to defend the status quo, or at least not challenge it publicly in any but a diffident way, became evident during his first year as bishop.

Violence against dissidents was on the rise in El Salvador around the time Romero was appointed Bishop of Santiago de María. Much of it was perpetrated by the national guard and ORDEN (*Organización Democrática Nacionalista*), an intelligence-gathering arm of the government that recruited, either voluntarily or forcibly, *campesinos* and other rural civilians to spy on their neighbors and report any "subversive" activities. ORDEN quickly outstripped its original mission of surveillance and became a forerunner of the death squads which terrorized the nation by kidnapping, torturing, and murdering anyone considered to be a Communist or Communist sympathizer. One of those death squads would assassinate Romero in 1980.

In 1974, a number of brutalities were perpetrated against *campesinos* in several rural areas. Just two weeks before Romero moved to Santiago de María, six *campesinos* were murdered in the hamlet of La Cayetana. A half-year later, in May 1975, a parish priest from Tecoluca was kidnapped and beaten by national guardsmen. The forces of repression were growing bolder in their retaliatory measures against clergy they considered meddlesome.

Then, on June 21, guardsmen attacked Tres Calles, a hamlet in Romero's own diocese. Beginning shortly after midnight, they raided a few houses, pulled five *campesinos* out into the open air, and hacked them to death with machetes.

Accompanied by a Passionist priest, Romero visited the site of the massacre the next morning. He spoke with the grieving survivors, saw the corpse of one of the victims, and interviewed others who had been beaten during the nighttime attack. At one point, an already rattled Romero was startled when a squad of guardsmen headed toward him as he walked through the village. To his relief, they passed by without interfering with him. When he and his Passionist companion were driving away from Tres Calles, a somber Romero said, "Father, we have to find a way to evangelize the rich, so that they change, so that they convert!"[3]

Romero followed up by protesting to the local commander of the national guard, who not only shrugged off the incident but actually had the effrontery to issue a veiled threat to Romero: "Cassocks are not bulletproof!"[4] So the bishop, now more angry than frightened, sat down to write President Molina.

"I am fulfilling my duty as Diocesan Bishop," he began, "by expressing to you my respectful but firm protest for the way in which a 'security force' illegitimately claims the right to kill and mistreat." It was a good start. But then Romero went on in an almost obsequious way to assure the president that he wasn't defending those who had been killed—for all he knew, they were guilty of crimes—but only protesting their extrajudicial executions. He made it clear that his motives were entirely "pastoral," and that, confident as he was in the president's "personal values," he was sure that the massacre at Tres Calles would be investigated. Finally, he told Molina that he had no intention of making a public statement about the incident, having "no desire for the limelight."[5]

The deferential letter was sent to the president by special courier. There was no response, nor was there any investigation into the atrocity. Yet Romero still wasn't ready to acknowledge that El Salvador's woes were the result of systemic inequality and institutional sin rather than the individual actions of rogue guardsmen.

Romero's timidity in not publicly calling out the perpetrators of the murders didn't go unnoticed. One of the attendees at the Ninth Day Memorial Mass Romero celebrated for the Tres Calles victims recalled how disgusted he and others were by the bishop's elegy. "That Monseñor Romero made me mad," he said. "He was so wishy-washy! He talked about 'the dead' instead of the people who had been 'murdered,' and he preached a sermon condemning violence, which practically suggested that those poor men had been killed because they were violent, that they somehow had it coming to them."[6]

Despite his sympathy for them, Romero continued for some time to blame the victims of oppression, seeing them as ideologically driven disrupters who often hid behind and misused the Gospel. This became clear in his clash just a month later with Los Naranjos ("Orange Grove"), a teaching and retreat center run by Passionist priests.

Its purpose, in keeping with Medellín, was to train *campesinos* as delegates of the Word for base communities. President Molina's government as well as Emanuele Gerada, the papal nuncio to El Salvador, considered the center a hotbed of subversion where illiterate field hands were hoodwinked into mistaking Marxist ideology for Christianity. Authorities already had detained one of its founders, a priest named Juan Macho Merino, and deported him (temporarily, as it turned out) back to his native Spain.

Of particular concern was a course offered at the center called "National Reality" which examined the history of El Salvador, the socioeconomic gap between the wealthy elites and everyone else, and the need for agrarian reform. Romero, already ambivalent about the center, took the time to sit in on a couple of sessions and found them too political. But when Macho was arrested, Romero immediately protested to government officials and eventually managed to have the ban against him lifted.

Still, it wasn't long before Romero closed the center down. In late July, 1975, a group of students protested the government's shutdown of the Autonomous University of Santa Ana. National guardsmen sent in to quell the demonstration wound up shooting forty or so of the protesters, provoking outrage throughout the nation. A group of students and priests, one of whom was associated with Los Naranjos, occupied the cathedral in San Salvador. Even during his three years as archbishop when he protected dissidents against government security forces and death squads, Romero was never comfortable with protesters occupying Church buildings. But in 1975 he was entirely unsympathetic to it. So he took the Passionist priest's participation as an excuse to shut down Los Naranjos until he had time to reassess the center's status.

His move angered Fr. Victorino Sevilla, the Passionist regional vicar for Central America, who traveled from his headquarters in Honduras to lay an ultimatum before Romero: Either support the work of the center or the Passionists would pack up and move to another diocese. Given the fact that he had but twenty-odd aging priests to minister to a staggering number of lay Catholics, Romero wasn't eager to lose the services, which included basic literacy and first aid instruction, offered by Los Naranjos. But neither was he willing to give his stamp of approval to the center's core curriculum, especially the "National Reality" course.

So a compromise was reached that allowed the center's work to continue, albeit in different form. The political and sociological thrust of its curriculum was toned down, and actual instruction was conducted at the parish level under the watchful supervision of parish priests and Romero. As a conciliatory gesture, Romero made Fr. Macho his educational vicar for the entire diocese.

Many people, including most of the Passionists, suspected that Romero's handling of Los Naranjos was motivated more by spite than anything else. But his temporary closure and restructuring of it impressed the papal nuncio so much that he pushed for Romero to become the next archbishop of El Salvador. At the same time, however, it is also the case that Romero's exposure to the center's mission, and especially his working relationship and eventual friendship with Macho, began to alter his opinion of both Medellín and the base community movement. It wasn't long before Romero was praising *campesino* catechists in his sermons and articles. This was a big step in his evolution as the spiritual and moral leader of the Salvadoran people.

Around this same time there was another event that began to change Romero's thinking: the publication of *Evangelii Nuntiandi*, "On Evangelization in the Modern World," an apostolic exhortation by Pope Paul VI. Paul was greatly admired and loved by Romero, who saw him as a personal role model. As a priest of the Roman Catholic Church, Romero was already disposed to take the words of a pope seriously. But what Paul said took on a special importance precisely because Romero so respected him.

In his exhortation, Paul offered direction on methods of evangelization that he believed would appeal to the modern temperament. The document is often credited with being the inauguration of the New Evangelization movement that became such an essential feature of St. John Paul II's pontificate, because in it Paul offers counsel on how to revitalize Catholic individuals and groups grown tepid in their commitment to the faith. One of the ways of doing this, the pope suggested, is to encourage the growth of base communities.

Paul recognized that not all base communities strengthen the Body of Christ, and he specifically warned against those which "come together in a spirit of bitter criticism of the Church, which they are quick to stigmatize as 'institutional' and to which they set themselves up in opposition as charismatic communities, free from structures and inspired only by the Gospel." Such communities, the pope warned, "very quickly become ideological" and "fall victim to some political option or current of thought."[7] This was exactly Romero's fear.

But, the pope continued, base communities led by trained laypersons can be invaluable when they gather together people for the purpose of "listening to and meditating on the Word" and empower one another "to be united in the struggle for justice, brotherly aid to the poor, [and] human advancement." Then they not only enable people to "live the Church's life more intensely," but also address the hunger for "a more human dimension" that larger and more traditional ecclesial structures may not be able to provide.[8]

Even more influentially for Romero, Pope Paul explicitly called out the economic and social injustices that were the focus of both Medellín and the Passionist-run Los Naranjos center. He insisted that it was "impossible" to accept an approach to evangelization that ignored the urgency of "the problems so much discussed today concerning justice, liberation, development and peace in the world. This would be to forget the lesson which comes to us from the Gospel concerning love of our neighbor who is suffering and in need."[9]

Just a month before the release of *Evangelii Nuntiandi,* Romero had written a memorandum for the Pontifical Commission for Latin America that spelled out his own take on what he called the "priests' political movement in El Salvador." In it, he seemed unwilling to acknowledge, as Pope Paul soon did in his apostolic exhortation, that some base communities could be legitimate centers of evangelization and that nonviolent support of liberation struggles can be perfectly compatible with the Gospel.

In his memo, Romero argued that there were three factors in the "politicization"—code for "corruption"—of Salvadoran centers like Los Naranjos.

The first was the baneful influence of liberal Jesuits at the Central American University. He singled out Ignacio Ellacuría, who would be brutally murdered by a death squad fourteen years later, and implicated without naming another Jesuit, liberation theologian Jon Sobrino. As far as Romero was concerned, they and other members of the Society of Jesus were peddling Communist propaganda.

The second factor Romero singled out as toxic was an interdiocesan justice and peace commission that published a bulletin which, he maintained, encouraged a "politicizing and contestational tendency" contrary to Church teaching. That the commission was warmly supported by Romero's old rival Bishop Rivera only deepened his distrust of it.

Finally, Romero targeted base communities themselves as cells in which radical priests propagated their subversive message to stir up discontent among the *campesinos*.[10]

Romero was honest enough to admit in his memorandum that El Salvador suffered under a cruelly repressive government bent on maintaining and protecting a concentration of wealth among a very few people. But he was convinced that the Church's role in responding to the situation had to remain apolitical. As he had insisted again and again throughout his years in San Salvador, the Church's responsibility—and his, as a leader in the Church—was to make sure that clergy kept their focus on the spiritual needs of rich and poor alike, trusting that the first could be converted by gentle persuasion and the second consoled by faith.

Despite the memo's self-assured tone, it soon became clear, especially after *Evangelii Nuntiandi* appeared, that Romero was increasingly conflicted in his attitude. On the one hand, he came from humble beginnings and in his pastoral work, as far back as the famine-stricken war years in Rome, he had always had a special place in his heart for the poor. On the other hand, he was a *romanità* respecter of both state and Church authority, and his innate timidity made it extremely difficult for him to buck either. Moreover, he was flattered by, and hence reluctant to damage, what he mistakenly supposed was a close personal relationship with the nation's elite. In time he would come to realize that, with the exception of Rafael Valladares, all the friends in high places he presumed he had remained so only as long as he defended the status quo from which they benefited.

Slowly, though, a change was taking place in Romero during his two years in Santiago de María. President Molina's apparent indifference to the Tres Calles massacre had begun to chip away at his confidence that the nation's political leaders could be converted. And a closer examination of the wealthy landowners' treatment of *campesinos* cast doubt upon them as well. During his Santiago de María episcopacy, a Passionist priest angrily told Romero that the local landowners were cheating *campesinos* by paying them less than the legally required daily minimum wage of 2.50 *colóns*—about one US dollar—by designating new hires as "picker's helpers" undeserving of a full wage. Romero refused to believe him, so the Passionist took the bishop to a sign posted on one of the plantations that brazenly announced "Here we pay 1.75 *colóns* a day." With unemployment so high in the diocese, the wealthy could easily find *campesinos* desperate enough for work to settle for subminimum wages.

In his first year in Santiago de María, Romero had been scan-dalized when protesting students and priests occupied the San Salvador cathedral. In his second year, he willingly threw open the doors of a Catholic high school as well as rooms in his own lodgings to shelter indigent coffee harvesters who had no place other than the streets to sleep during the cold autumn nights. He also made sure that Catholic charity organizations such as Caritas supplied the pickers with a hot meal or drink each night.

Despite his rocky start with the priests who ran Los Naranjos, they slowly helped him appreciate that his attitude to *campesinos* had been distorted and patronizing. Romero had assumed that they were too unschooled and coarse to be capable of learning, much less teaching, the Bible. His longstanding respect for authority inclined him to stick with a hierarchical view of society in which each class had its own designated function, and preaching the Word of God definitely wasn't a task proper to laypersons. Base community education of the peasant class threatened to upset that orderly structure, thrusting field hands into tasks for which they were unsuited by nature and custom.

Romero's growing friendship with the Passionist priest Fr. Macho punctured this bias by showing him firsthand just how wise *campesino* interpretations of Scripture could be. One story told by Macho illustrates Romero's growing appreciation.

At a base community Gospel discussion to which Macho had taken him, Romero listened to a young *campesino* reflecting on the story of the loaves and fishes. At one point, the youth said that the discussion had helped him understand that "the boy who carried the five loaves and two fishes in his bag was the one who really obligated Christ to perform the miracle." Romero, skep-tical and looking for an opportunity to instruct, pounced. "Young man," he snipped. "Why do you think that anyone could obligate Christ to do anything?"

But the *campesino* was up to the challenge. He explained to Romero that because the boy offered everything he had in giving the loaves and fishes, "Jesus could do no less. He had to do everything he could, too. And he could do miracles! So he did!"[11]

According to Macho, Romero was so impressed that his doubts about the ability of the *campesinos* to interpret the Gospels vanished or at least significantly lessened.

In mid-1976, President Molina surprised the nation by announcing that his government was ready to undertake agrarian reform intended to redistribute farm land that had been concentrated for generations in the hands of a few Salvadoran families. Specifically, Molina proposed that the government purchase 150,000 acres of good farmland at market price from landowners, some of whom didn't even live in El Salvador, and redistribute them to 12,000 landless families.

Romero, who in his San Salvador period had expressed doubts about such a redistribution, was excited by the reform proposals and organized a three-day seminar for priests in his diocese to study them. Ruben Zamora, an expert on agrarian reform, led the discussions, and Romero sat with his priests carefully listening and taking copious notes. Zamora was struck by how eager the bishop was to absorb every last bit of information he could. "The man," he remembered, "wanted to learn."[12]

At the end of the seminar, an enthusiastic Romero conveyed to Molina his priests' feedback on the proposed reform. It was all in vain, however, because the president soon bowed to the landowners' furious resistance and quashed the entire enterprise. Romero was shocked. He'd assumed that Molina had been serious and that the plantation owners would act decently by sharing some of their land at no real loss to themselves so that the horrible levels of poverty in El Salvador might be reduced. It was yet another step in his awakening.

In his weekly columns for the diocesan newspaper *El Apóstol,* Romero for the most part had stuck to relatively innocuous topics that steered clear of political commentary or social criticism. Yet his two years in Santiago had awakened him to the fact that the plight of landless farmworkers wasn't part of the natural order of things decreed by God, but instead was spawned by laws and social institutions that favored the wealthy. In a piece written just two months before he was named archbishop of San Salvador, Romero let it be known that his thinking had changed. In blasting the "human sin" of greed that "makes the beauty of creation groan," he wrote, "it saddens and troubles us to see the selfishness with which ways and means are found to cancel out the coffee pickers' just wage." And then he quoted a passage from the Letter of James that foreshadowed the three-year crusade on which he was about to embark.

"Look! The wages you failed to pay the workers who mowed your fields are crying out against you. The cries of the harvesters have reached the ears of the Lord Almighty."[13]

CHAPTER SIX

Baptism

"You know, there is baptism by water, and there is baptism by blood. But there is also baptism by the people."[1]

By December 1976, Luis Chávez y González, seventy-five years old and archbishop of San Salvador for half his life, was too tired and disillusioned to continue. He was ready to hand over the burdens of office to someone else.

Since Medellín, he had seen the Salvadoran oligarchy's repression of "subversive" *campesinos* skyrocket. Because of the increasingly vocal clerical awareness that the nation's troubles stemmed from institutional injustice, attacks against the Church, hitherto nearly unheard of, were also on the rise. Foreign-born priests were especially targeted for arrest, torture, and deportation. But Salvadoran ones were also at risk, and the archdiocesan printing press offices, a Catholic bookstore, and the Central American University had all been bombed, almost certainly on direct orders or unofficial nods from the government. President Molina had stopped accepting calls from Chávez. He was tired of hearing the archbishop protest the escalating violence.

Worst of all, only one of his bishops, Rivera, agreed with Chávez's embrace of Medellín's vision. The others, including Romero, were still convinced that calling out economic and social injustice was the job of politicians, not churchmen. To meddle in such things was to betray the Gospel by turning it into a political instrument.

Given their collaborative relationship, Chávez wanted Rivera to succeed him and lobbied the Vatican mightily for his appointment. But papal nuncio Gerada had been busy behind the scenes undermining Chávez. Anticipating the aged archbishop's retirement, Gerada, an ardent foe of Medellín, wanted Chávez's replacement to be someone who would steer clear of rocking the social, political, and economic boat. After consulting with forty of the nation's prime movers and shakers, he concluded that the safest successor to Chávez was Romero, widely known as a conciliator and easily manipulatable appeaser. When Chávez got the news, it felt like a slap in the face. "It's curious that the [Vatican] paid no attention to me regarding Monseñor Rivera, who was always my candidate and they knew it," he said. Then, plaintively, he added, "Forty years as archbishop and they didn't take my opinion into account."[2]

The official announcement of Romero's appointment was made on February 10, 1977. That same day, he gave an interview which must have gladdened the hearts of the nation's elite. Although the previous two years had opened his eyes to a certain extent to the nation's structural injustice, he still insisted that the Church had to keep to the center, mindful of the need for justice but focused primarily on traditional pastoral duties, not politics. Twelve days later, in a rather low-key ceremony, he was installed as the new archbishop of San Salvador. Afterward, Romero and the other bishops paid a courtesy call on President Molina who churlishly took the opportunity to lambast them for what he claimed was the Church's contribution to the national discontent. It was a misplaced display of pique, given that the bishops were more sympathetic than not to the interests of landowners and political leaders.

In his new position as the Catholic primate of El Salvador, Romero soon discovered that it was a vexing time to be charged with overseeing the nation's spiritual well-being. His country was in a crisis that, during his three years as archbishop, only got worse, finally culminating almost immediately after his death in bloody civil war.

Having no mineral resources to fall back on, El Salvador's economy had always relied on exporting cash crops like coffee, cotton, and sugarcane. As we've already seen, one result of this was a massive maldistribution of arable land. When Romero became archbishop, just 2 percent of the country's population owned 60 percent of cultivatable land. Because half of the remaining 40 percent was too mountainous or rocky to farm, this left the rest of the population with just 20 percent of the arable land. Another way of looking at this is equally unsettling: 20 percent of the population accounted for 66 percent of the GNP, while the poorest 20 percent produced less than 2 percent.

The national norm, consequently, was unemployment and grinding poverty for most of the population, and incredible wealth, privilege, and power for a tiny handful. This in turn led to an acceleration of *campesino* resistance to the status quo, much of it inspired by the 1959 success of the Castro revolution in Cuba and further fueled by the Salvadoran government's progressively harsh crackdown on domestic dissent. The 1979 success of the Sandinista-led revolution in Nicaragua would also soon encourage Salvadoran reformers and rebels.

The cruel irony behind the disparity in El Salvador's distribution of wealth is that the nation's economy had actually been growing in the twenty years leading up to Romero's installation as archbishop. Thanks in part to a booming market for the cash crops El Salvador sold—by this time the coffee market had recovered from its 1930s crash—but also to a concerted effort on the part of government and business to sell the nation as a hot tourist spot, the GNP rose at an average annual rate of over 5 percent in the 1960s and over 6 percent in the 1970s. The trouble was that nearly none of the additional wealth trickled down. The rich got much richer, and the poor much, much poorer.

There was another reason for the nation's economic growth during this period. It had become a player in the Cold War, with the United States monitoring it closely out of fear that social instability made it ripe for a Communist takeover. Even before outright civil war erupted in 1980, the administration of US President Jimmy Carter was bankrolling the Salvadoran military as well as training national guardsmen and future death squad members in the infamous School of the Americas at Fort Benning, Georgia. The aid would increase exponentially in President Ronald Reagan's campaign to forestall the dreaded and largely fictitious domino effect in Latin America.

Brazilian bishop Dom Hélder Câmara, who resisted economic and political oppression in his own country, was noted for his "spiral of violence" analysis of conflict perpetuation. The economic and physical violence sanctioned by a ruling power to retain its dominance, he argued, gives rise to proportionate responses on the part of those who are oppressed. This only ratchets up the violence of the government, which in turn elevates the violence of resisters. Before long, the violence from both sides has spiraled out of control, embroiling everyone in a furious maelstrom of destruction.

El Salvador at the time Romero became archbishop was a case study of Dom Hélder's thesis. The government, egged on by US Cold War fears as well as its own anxieties about a slippage of power, began a systematic campaign of terror to discourage dissent. National guardsmen, ORDEN members, and thuggish assassins who belonged to a clandestine and brutal group pretentiously calling itself the White Warriors Union rampaged through cities and rural areas in search of suspected subversives. They frequently raped, mutilated, and murdered innocent men and women, and sometimes even children, in hideous ways designed to terrorize and deter other dissenters.

In response to these atrocities, resistance groups originally formed to lobby for *campesino* civil rights, unions, fairer wages, and agrarian reform frequently morphed into full-fledged guerrilla militias that met fire with fire. Although their tactics were generally less cruel than the military's, they committed their share of murders and regularly kidnapped wealthy Salvadorans to finance their resistance. Romero condemned the violence committed by both sides in the conflict and, consistent with his Christian faith, urged them to find nonviolent ways to arrive at peace with justice. But his pleas went largely unheeded by the combatants.

Romero's call for an end to the killing was ignored by guerrillas and military alike for the same reason: the Salvadoran Church's longstanding support of the economic and political ruling class. The guerrillas, embittered by generations of ecclesial silence about the systematic injustice and inequality that crippled the majority of Salvadorans, were unwilling to trust any call for peace that came from a churchman. To their ears, it sounded like just another pious pie-in-the-sky subterfuge that favored the status quo.

To the wealthy elite who had long supported the Salvadoran Church financially and in turn expected the Church's public support, even mild clerical criticisms of governmental and military brutality came across as betrayals, and their fury soon expanded to include all Catholic clerics. It's not that the elite were particularly religious. But they had relied on the Church to justify their privileged positions and to placate the poor by urging patience and humility. Once that alliance was jeopardized, they responded with vehement anticlericalism. Priests were denounced as Communist agitators who threatened the nation's security. In Romero's first six months as archbishop, there were no fewer than sixty-two newspaper ads, written and paid for by the oligarchy, condemning the Church. They in turn spawned over thirty sympathetic editorials in papers across the nation. Spray-painted onto public walls and printed on leaflets was a horrifying slogan that became all too familiar during these years: *Haga patria, mate a un cura:* "Be a patriot, kill a priest."

As the national guard commander had warned Romero when he protested the 1975 Tres Calles massacre, cassocks were not bulletproof.

The turmoil that had become the Salvadoran norm erupted yet again the very week that Romero was installed as archbishop. National elections had been held on February 20. President Molina had been dropped by the ruling party because of his attempt at agrarian reform. Instead, the establishment candidate was General Carlos Humberto Romero (no relation to the archbishop), running against a reform candidate from the coalition party UNO, which had victory stolen from it in the 1972 election. Massive ballot fraud and voter intimidation handed the election to Romero.

The losing candidate, a retired cavalry officer, promptly proclaimed the election the latest example of governmental corruption and announced he would stage a demonstration in San Salvador's Plaza Libertad to demand an honest recount. He was joined by as many as 40,000 to 60,000 disgruntled fellow citizens. Workers throughout the city staged strikes and workplace shutdowns in solidarity with them.

The crowds remained in the plaza for three days, finally beginning to disperse on the last evening following an outdoor mass. Shortly after midnight on February 27, troops surrounded the square and the 6,000 remaining protesters were ordered to leave within ten minutes. At the end of that time, the soldiers opened fire on the 1,500 or so who remained. Those who could fled panic-stricken to a nearby church, seeking sanctuary and safety.

The newly appointed archbishop was nowhere to be seen. Romero had returned to the Diocese of Santiago de María to wrap things up there. He was informed by telephone that trouble was brewing even before the shooting in the square began and urged to return to San Salvador in the hope that his presence would inhibit an outbreak of violence. Instead, according to the person who made the phone call, Romero said that he would pray for everyone involved, and then rang off.[3] It fell to former Archbishop Chávez and Bishop Rivera to intervene with the military so that the protesters inside the church could leave unharmed. The number of people killed in the plaza on that terrible night is still uncertain, but estimates are upward of three hundred.

Romero did return to San Salvador later that day and was briefed by Chávez and Rivera about what had happened. Even while he was still absorbing the shocking news, the violence accelerated. Guardsmen tried to arrest a "Red" priest in a village not far from the capital but were prevented from doing so when courageous parishioners gathered to block the soldiers' entry. An American priest working in the country was expelled, and seven other priests who were out of the country were refused reentry.

The Salvadoran bishops conference convened the week after the Plaza Libertad tragedy to draft a public response to this latest surge of violence. Romero toned down some of its language, and even at the last minute worried that it was too strong. But Bishop Rivera managed to persuade him that troubled times called for boldly prophetic proclamations.

In the document, the bishops announced that the "basic sin" they were called to address as leaders of the Church was the injustice infecting El Salvador's "political, social, and economic order." They pointed out, in the spirit of Medellín's preferential option for the poor principle, that the Salvadorans who suffered most from unjust institutions were those already most at risk: the landless and poor *campesinos* "who must struggle day to day in order to survive, who live in habitual unemployment and with a hunger that debases them to the direst levels of undernourishment."[4] The drafting of the document was the last time the Salvadoran bishops would present a united front to the government.

The plan was for Romero to read the statement during his homily on Sunday, March 13. Because the service would be broadcast by radio stations, the message would get out to a large audience. But a tragedy that occurred the day before disrupted that plan. It also irrevocably propelled Romero headlong in the spiritual and pastoral direction he had slowly and tentatively been headed for the last couple of years. It was a definite tipping point in his life.

His good friend Rutilio Grande, the only Jesuit in El Salvador with whom Romero had a close relationship at the time, was brutally murdered.

Given Romero's ongoing feud with the Jesuits, his friendship with Grande is perplexing at first glance. But they actually had a lot in common. Both were born in rural towns to families of modest means. As youngsters, both dressed up like priests and played at leading religious processions and celebrating Mass. Both were awkwardly shy children, preferring to pray in their local church to playing football with other kids.

The two of them shared something else, too: They both suffered from psychological anxiety and religious scrupulosity. Romero, it will be recalled, traced his own nervous afflictions to an insecure childhood. Grande's early years were much worse than Romero's. His parents separated when he was still a boy, leaving him to be raised by a very devout grandmother. The psychological wounds created by this early trauma led to or at least exacerbated several psychological crises later in his life.

Upon graduating from the seminary of San José de la Montaña in 1945, Grande joined the Society of Jesus. As part of his training, he was sent to Ecuador and Panama, where he studied as well as taught. It was there, in 1950, that he suffered what appears to have been a psychotic breakdown, perhaps brought on most immediately by his heavy workload. Grande fell into a state that alternated between catatonic-like withdrawal and frantic gibbering. Although he eventually recovered, a similar attack befell him the following year, raising some question among his superiors about whether he was stable enough to continue in Jesuit formation. But the decision was eventually made to retain him. So Grande was sent to Spain to teach and was ordained there in 1959—an event that once again sent him into a psychological tailspin from which it took months to recover.

In the mid-1960s Grande spent a few months studying at the Lumen Vitae Institute in Belgium, immersing himself in the writings and spirit of the Second Vatican Council's reforms. When he returned to El Salvador in 1967 to teach at San José de la Montaña, he was afire with a vision of the Church that made room for all the People of God. The following year, he enthusiastically embraced Medellín's recommendation of a preferential option for the poor, and often spoke of it in the courses he taught at the seminary.

It wasn't long after his return to El Salvador that Grande met Romero. Despite the ten-year difference in their ages, the two hit it off right away, often taking long walks together, sharing memories of their childhoods, and discussing their vision and hopes for the Church, which at that time significantly differed.

Grande made no secret of his commitment to a Church that took the struggle for justice as an integral part of its Gospel proclamation. His outspoken endorsement of Medellín so rankled the more traditionally minded Salvadoran bishops that they vetoed his nomination to become rector of the seminary in 1972. Disillusioned and depressed, perhaps teetering on the edge of another breakdown, Grande left the seminary to teach high school. But he was rejuvenated after spending some time at the Latin American Pastoral Institute in Quito, Ecuador, an internationally known center that specialized in teaching liberation theology and training clerics and laypeople alike in Christ-centered service to the poor. When he returned to El Salvador, Grande decided to give up teaching and devote himself to parish work—an unusual move at the time for a Salvadoran Jesuit. He was assigned to the city of Aguilares and its surrounding villages, one of which was Grande's hometown of El Paisnal.

Along with some like-minded priests, Grande launched a new style of ministry that stretched ecclesial conventions to the breaking point. He dressed in civilian clothes, often the same linen shirt and pants, rope sandals, and straw hat worn by *campesinos*, insisted on being called "Tilo" (short for Rutilio) instead of "Father," and made a point of visiting his parishioners and sharing their modest meals instead of waiting for them to come to him. He encouraged the formation of base communities to teach peasants to read, hear, and discuss the Gospels, understand them, and seek their relevance to their own situations and problems. He wanted them to be Christians with voices, not silent sufferers, so that they could take active rolls in working for social and economic reform and their own liberation.

Grande's ministry to the *campesinos* became increasingly irksome to landowners in the vicinity of Aguilares. One of them, Eduardo Orellana, was killed in December 1976 during a rancorous encounter with members of a couple of *campesino* unions, the Christian Federation of Salvadoran Peasants (FECCAS) and the Farm Workers' Union (UTC). Shots rang out, and Orellana was hit, perhaps by friendly fire from his own brother. But Orellana's fellow landowners insisted he'd been killed by the unionists and used his death as an opportunity to launch a campaign of calumny against Grande and other priests they accused of Communist sympathies.

One month later, doubtlessly in the hope of intimidating Grande and his coworkers, national guardsmen kidnapped, beat, and deported a Colombian priest who also worked with rural peasants establishing base communities. But the tactic backfired, because Grande and dozens of others gathered in Apopa, the town where the priest had served, for a peaceful protest. At the Mass that climaxed the demonstration, Grande delivered a homily that unambiguously threw down the gauntlet. He argued that El Salvador was full of "Cains" and "Abels," the first being the powerful elite, the second being the *campesinos* who were tortured, killed, or disappeared when they stood up for their human rights. He singled out participants in base communities as especially in peril because, he said, to learn and preach the Gospel was a dangerous challenge to the nation's Cains. Soon, Grande predicted, the politicians and oligarchs would get rid of every Bible in the land, ripping out their contents and leaving only covers. And he reminded his hearers that "in Christianity, one must be willing to give his or her life in service for a just order, in order to save others, for the values of the Gospel."[5]

With these words, Grande sealed his own fate. Exactly one month later, as he drove with four companions, two of them young children, to celebrate Mass in his hometown, his car was ambushed and he and the two adults accompanying him were slaughtered. The terrified children were allowed to go free, and it was they who carried the grisly news to Grande's Aguilares parishioners. The three corpses were retrieved and brought to the parish church. Grande had been hit with so many bullets that one of the people who saw his body said it looked almost disintegrated.

Later that day, Romero received a phone call from President Molina telling him about the murder, assuring him—falsely—that the government had no hand in it. He promised a thorough investigation. Romero, shocked to his very core, set out immediately for Aguilares and arrived there around 10 p.m. When he saw the bloodied corpses, the change wrought in him was later called by some "Rutilio's miracle."[6] According to Jesuit theologian Jon Sobrino, a priest with whom Romero had sparred in earlier years and who was present that day in Aguilares, "The will of God must have looked very different to Archbishop Romero that night in the presence of those three bodies and with hundreds of *campesinos* staring at him wondering what he was going to do about what had happened."[7]

Archbishop Chávez, who had befriended Grande when he was still a boy and encouraged him to enter the priesthood, also came to Aguilares when he received news of the murder. The old man collapsed with grief when he saw Grande's corpse. So Romero and another priest celebrated an impromptu memorial Mass for the three slain men, who were buried two days later.

Over the objections of the papal nuncio, Romero cancelled the regular curricula of the parochial schools throughout the country to give teachers and students an opportunity to discuss the accelerating national unrest. He also declared a *misa única* or single nationwide Mass for the following Sunday, March 20. Issuing to the faithful a dispensation from the obligation to attend Mass in their own parishes, he urged Catholics throughout the land to make their way to San Salvador for Grande's funeral, to be held at the cathedral. For those who couldn't physically be there, the Mass would be broadcast by radio to every village and hamlet. One hundred thousand people showed up, filling the plaza and streets that surrounded the cathedral. As they listened to Romero's homily, he assured them—and at the same time warned the government—that "as Christ's humble successor and representative here in the archdiocese: the one who attacks one of my priests, attacks me."[8]

At that very moment Romero, like his friend Rutilio, threw down the gauntlet. He put the government and oligarchy on notice that he was God's servant, not theirs.

After the *misa única*, Romero paid a personal visit to President Molina, who once again assured him that the government was investigating the three murders. But Romero went away convinced that Molina was lying to him and vowed to boycott governmental functions until an investigation was actually launched. It never was, and for the next three years, the archbishop of San Salvador was noticeably absent from all official state gatherings.

What exactly was the "Rutilio miracle" that happened to Romero on the day Grande was murdered? Many, including Jon Sobrino, have interpreted the event as a kind of road-to-Damascus conversion, an abrupt change of allegiance from a traditional and timid view of priesthood to a wholehearted embrace of the Gospel of liberation advocated by Medellín and, in a less dramatic fashion, by Pope Paul VI in his *Evangelii Nuntiandi*.

But this seems overly romanticized. Such spontaneous conversions are rare, and it's even rarer that they abide. In Romero's case, it's much more likely that Grande's death was the final straw in a long process of coming to terms with the time and place in which God had called him to serve. Romero had always been concerned for the welfare of the poor, even though his bureaucratic years in San Salvador had taken him away from direct contact with them. When he resumed pastoral duties as Bishop of Santiago de María, he did so with a growing awareness of the root causes of *campesino* misery. Even though he balked at what he initially considered to be the excesses of Medellín, he'd long accepted, even if somewhat abstractly, Vatican II's conclusion that it was the Church's responsibility to minister to the material as well as the spiritual needs of the People of God. The ugly examples of El Salvador's repressive government and greedy oligarchy incrementally encouraged him to take a second look at the base community movement and the preferential option for the poor affirmed at Medellín. The murder of his friend Rutilio finally drew all these strands together to weave a fresh way of seeing and behaving in the world.

Romero himself never referred to that night in Aguilares as a conversion experience. Instead, he preferred to call it a "change of attitude" or "a development in the process of awareness." He spoke of the awakening of a "special pastoral *fortaleza*" or fortitude that enabled him to stand up to the forces of repression crippling El Salvador. "I believed in conscience," he wrote, "that God was calling me" to take a stand "that contrasted with my temperament and my 'conservative' inclinations." That call, he believed, awakened him to the "duty to take a positive stand to defend my Church and, on behalf of the Church, to stand with my greatly oppressed people."[9]

Still, the change in him was profound. Perhaps no one has better captured it than Jon Sobrino, even if we reject his claim about a sudden conversion. Romero, he points out, was fifty-nine years old at the time, "an age at which people's psychological and mental structure, their understanding of the faith, their spirituality, and their Christian commitment have typically hardened." Moreover, he'd just been made an archbishop, which easily could have reinforced his inclination toward a conservative *romanità* resistance to change within the Church. Finally, he knew that he'd been chosen as archbishop by the nation's elite who expected him to reciprocate by "revers[ing] the line taken by his predecessor, Luis Chávez y González."[10] Yet, remarkably, none of these factors inhibited Romero from following the ministerial path Grande's death revealed to him.

If *conversion* isn't the best word to describe Romero's change in attitude and activities, a more appropriate one, suggests Romero's fellow priest and friend José Inocencio Alas, might be *baptism*. In adult baptism, we put away the old self and put on the Christ-self, but only after a long preparatory period of meditation, prayer, and self-examination. Everything in Romero's life up to that horrible night in March 1977 prepared him, as Alas said, to "cross the threshold. He went through the door. Because, as you know, there is baptism by water, and there is baptism by blood. But there is also baptism by the people."[11] As Romero stood over Grande's shattered body that night in Aguilares, he finally and fully embraced what God wanted from him. And when they sensed the change in him, the *campesinos* whom he served baptized him with their tears and their love.

CHAPTER SEVEN

A Paschal Church

"You are Christ today, suffering in history."[1]

In the weeks following Grande's murder, a reversal occurred in Romero's life that must have delighted as well as disconcerted him.

On the one hand, his strong denunciations of Grande's assassination and the power imbalance in El Salvador that allowed such atrocities to occur surprised priests and laypeople alike who had long disdained him as a timid and acquiescent puppet of the ruling class. They remained wary of him for a few more months, but soon grew to trust and love him, and Romero them.

On the other hand, his former allies, members of the powerful clique that ran the Salvadoran government, economy, and Church, turned against him for precisely the same reason that the priests and *campesinos* came to adore him. The pliable churchman whom they had expected to be an untroublesome archbishop turned out quite otherwise. They furiously believed he had double-crossed them by casting his lot with what they considered to be the Communist-infiltrated Medellín crowd.

To make matters worse, Romero's own bishops—Edwardo Alvarez, who was also the nation's military vicar, Benjamin Barrera, Pedro Arnoldo Aparacio, and Marco Revelo—believed he had gone too far, and throughout his entire tenure as arch-bishop regularly opposed his policies and wishes. Along with government officials and oligarchs, they accused him of confusing pastoral and political activities. The only bishop whom Romero could count on for moral and practical support was his onetime rival Arturo Rivera.

Finally, Romero had made a powerful enemy of Emanuele Gerada, papal nuncio to El Salvador, by overriding his objections to the *misa única*.

The new archbishop was savvy enough when it came to Church politics to know that the Roman curia would soon be deluged with complaints from all of his critics. So he decided to fly to Rome to present his own side of the story. Accompanied by two companions, Romero arrived there on March 26, a fortnight after Grande's murder. Only a few weeks into his new office, he was already worried that the curia was planning to strip him of the archdiocese. He knew he had to make a persuasive case.

After praying at St. Peter's and spending some meditative time before the tomb of his beloved Pius XI, Romero went directly to the superior general of the Society of Jesus, the Spaniard Pedro Arrupe. Although he had sparred with Jesuits in the past, he wanted to mend fences with the nearly sixty members of the society in El Salvador and hoped that a face-to-face meeting with their leader might begin the process. Romero also felt that he needed to give Arrupe a full account of Grande's murder.

While in Rome, he called on officials in the Congregation for Bishops and Vatican Secretariat of State to neutralize as best he could the negative appraisals of him coming in from Gerada. He wasn't too successful. He was roundly scolded at the secretariat and admonished to exemplify the prudence displayed by Jesus in his public ministry. An exasperated Romero replied, "If he was so prudent, then why was he killed?" Somewhat lamely, he was told that Jesus would've been killed sooner had he not shown as much prudence as he did.[2]

Disconcerting as this encounter was, Romero's audience with Paul VI, the pontiff he admired most after Pius XI, went well. Romero gave the pope a photograph of Grande and tried to convey some idea of the fraught situation in El Salvador for himself, his priests, and the Church. When he told Paul about the trouble he was having with his fellow Salvadoran bishops, the pope took hold of Romero's hands and said to him, "Courage! You are the one in charge!"[3]

Fr. César Jerez, one of the two men who traveled with Romero to the Eternal City, recollects that at one point during the visit he mustered the courage to say to him, "Monseñor, you've changed. What's happened?" His question was prompted by an awareness that Romero was newly afire with concern for the plight of Salvadoran *campesinos*.

Romero admitted that he'd been wondering about that as well and concluded that at least part of the change was sparked by his remembering what it had been like to grow up in a family that knew hunger. Because of "years and years" of study, and even more as a paper-pushing auxiliary bishop, he'd "started to forget where I came from." But his time as spiritual head of Santiago de María brought him once again into close contact with rural poverty and dredged up recollections of his own roots. "You know, Father," he said, "when a piece of charcoal has already been lit once, you don't have to blow on it much to get it to flame up again." The murder of his friend Rutilio, he concluded, was the breath that reignited the charcoal of his memories.[4]

The El Salvador Romero returned to on the eve of Palm Sunday was a nation where it had become acceptable and even patriotic to assault "Red" clergy verbally and, increasingly, physically. Romero's relationship with President Molina continued to deteriorate. The head of state escalated his accusations that the Church incited *campesino* unrest and he continued to stonewall on investigating Grande's murder. By the time he left office in July, thirty of Romero's priests had been assailed by the national guard or ORDEN. Some were beaten, tortured, or expelled, and two were murdered. A full 15 percent of San Salvador's active priests were affected by police and security force brutality.

Moreover, rural base communities were now openly targeted as Communist cells by security forces. Because delegates of the Word were especially viewed as threats, any peasant caught owning a Bible was in danger of a beating or worse. In some areas in the department of Chalatenango, simply going to Mass could get you killed. Dozens and then hundreds of people became *desaparecidos*, prisoners taken by the national guard who afterward vanished. Acts of terrorism became commonplace in the countryside.

The misery caused by all this was a major motive for Romero's first pastoral letter, released on Easter Sunday, April 10. Entitled "The Easter Church," it is the only one of Romero's four pastoral letters written entirely by himself. Probably begun before his trip to Rome, it was both an opportunity to organize his thoughts and an introductory communique to his people. It was also a testament, as he wrote in the letter, to his new understanding of his duty as a Christian leader that "the murder of the never-to-be-forgotten Father Rutilio Grande" had given him.[5]

The Church, wrote Romero, is the sacrament of Easter, a sign and instrument of the Risen Christ and hence of hope for fullness of life and salvation. The proper mission of the Church, therefore, is to avoid closing in on itself and turning its eyes from the world. It is called instead to "serve as Christ's instrument in the redemption of the whole of humanity."[6]

This is a perfectly traditional statement of the Church's purpose, and one that Romero endorsed throughout his entire priestly career. Up to that point, however, the redemption of all humanity had meant for him the conversion of the rich to acts of charity and the conversion of the poor to patience and forbearance. His first pastoral letter as archbishop reflected Romero's new appreciation of the connection between redemption, conversion, and liberation from material oppression, signaled by his repeated appeal to Medellín. "The Church in Latin America," he wrote, quoting from the Medellín conference's concluding document, "should be manifested, in an increasingly clear manner, as truly poor, missionary and paschal, separate from all temporal power and courageously committed to the liberation of each and every man." The Church, he continued, again quoting Medellín, "cannot be indifferent... when faced with 'a muted cry [that] pours from the throats of millions of men, asking their pastors for a liberation that reaches them from nowhere else.'"[7]

Romero concluded his letter by reaching out to El Salvador's political and wealthy elite, assuring them that he was always ready to dialogue. The Church, he wrote, "has been grateful when it could count upon them, just as it suffers when relationships have deteriorated." Fruitful conversation and collaboration with them is "one of the church's Easter hopes." But the archbishop also made his expectations of the nation's ruling class crystal-clear: "The political community and other elements of society need to be reminded that they are at the service of the personal and social vocation of men and women."[8]

In a homily delivered a month later, Romero went out of his way to proclaim that the Easter Church was the creature of neither the political right or left. "One side," he said, "accuses the church of being Marxist and subversive. Another group of people wants to reduce the church to a spirituality that is separated from the realities of the world, a type of preaching that remains in the clouds, that sings the psalms and prays, without any concern for earthly affairs." But the Easter Church, said Romero, preaches nonviolent liberation for all, rich and poor alike, and reserves for itself the right to pass moral judgment whenever human rights are violated.[9]

Less than a fortnight after the pastoral letter was released, Mauricio Borgonovo, foreign minister in Molina's government and a member of one of the nation's ruling families, was kidnapped by the insurgent group that called itself the Popular Liberation Forces (FPL). Romero's enemies insisted that his public criticisms of the government encouraged the act. Perhaps. But it's more likely that the FPL's motive was to bring home to the elite class the grief and fear felt by the families of *desaparecidos*. Its political goal was to force the government to release thirty-seven political prisoners in exchange for Borgonovo.

The very next day, a furious Molina ranted to Romero, his bishops, and the papal nuncio about the political activism of Salvadoran priests, especially the Jesuits, that encouraged groups like the FPL. Romero gave as good as he got, insisting that he had cautioned his clergy to be more mindful of their public pronouncements and that Molina needed to be less ready to label as subversive what was simply Vatican-approved teaching on social justice.

Nothing came of the heated meeting except a worsening of relations between the government and Romero. A week later, on May Day, government troops broke up labor union rallies in San Salvador. That same day, a Panama-born Jesuit who had worked with Grande in establishing base communities in the Aguilares region was arrested, beaten, and deported. Also arrested was a leader of the opposition coalition UNO. Just four days later, the archdiocesan printing office was bombed yet again.

In the meantime, Molina was taking a hard line with Borgonovo's kidnappers. He refused to negotiate with them, despite public pleas from the foreign minister's mother and Romero. The outcome was inevitable. On May 10, Borgonovo's body was found dumped on the side of a road. Because the slain foreign minister had been such an important Salvadoran, Romero said his funeral Mass. But the assembled elite who attended fumed with fury at the archbishop, whom they believed had to share responsibility for Borgonovo's murder.

They weren't the only ones enraged. The day of the funeral, an assassination team from the ultra-right White Warriors Union gunned down Alfonso Navarro, a young priest they mistook for a Jesuit, in retaliation for Borgonovo's killing. He and a teen-ager who happened to be with him were shot down in the parish rectory. Navarro, hit with at least seven bullets but still clinging to life, was rushed to a first aid station. The medical staff attending to him reported that he forgave his murderers before he died.

At Navarro's funeral, concelebrated with two hundred priests from all over El Salvador, Romero delivered one of his most memorable homilies. He told the story of a Bedouin guide trying to get a caravan of exhausted and thirsty travelers to an oasis. The travelers kept wanting to head toward mirages, and the guide kept telling them, "not that way—this way!" Increasingly frustrated and angry, they finally shot him. "And so," said Romero, "he died pointing the way. The legend becomes reality: a priest, pierced with bullets, who dies pardoning, who dies praying, gives his message to all of us." And that message? Reject violence. "Violence resolves nothing, violence is not Christian, not human."

Then Romero directed his remarks to President Molina, calling on him to investigate Navarro's murder with as much energy and conviction as he was devoting to tracking down the foreign minister's assassins. "The life of Mr. Borgonovo was sacred, but so was the life of the priest who is lost to us today, as was the life of Father Rutilio Grande."[10]

The murders of the statesman, priest, and teenager were gory preludes to what would prove to be a violent summer. The next atrocity occurred less than a week after Navarro's funeral in what the government called, in a deliberate attempt to provoke, "Operation Rutilio."

The area around Aguilares, Grande's home base, had long been viewed by the nation's ruling class as a seedbed of Jesuitical subversion. Now, five hundred *campesinos* who had been told to clear off of plots of lands they rented in El Paisnal, Grande's hometown situated close to Aguilares, refused to budge. On May 17, government troops moved in and evicted them at gunpoint. Many of them fled to Aguilares, which was surrounded by two thousand soldiers the following day.

After encircling the town, the soldiers went wild. They broke into homes, raped women and children, butchered at least fifty people on the spot—one of whom was shot simply because he tried to ring the church bell—and carted off hundreds more.

The three remaining Jesuits in Aguilares, all foreign-born, were arrested and promptly kicked out of the country.

Moreover, as a clear sign of contempt for the Church, the troops desecrated the town's church. They shot open its tabernacle, scattered the consecrated Hosts on the floor, and used the sanctuary as a barracks and base of operation.

As soon as he heard what had happened, Romero headed straight for Aguilares, but was refused permission to enter the town. The following day, after meeting with the interior minister and President Molina to protest the occupation, he issued a statement accusing the government of deliberate persecution of the Church flimsily "justified in the name of the struggle against atheistic Communism."[11] When Molina failed to respond to Romero's public challenge, the archbishop sent him a scathing letter that placed responsibility for what had happened squarely on his shoulders. Its tone and content clearly indicated Romero's intense anger and growing prophetic courage. "Mr. President, I cannot comprehend how, before the eyes of the nation, you can proclaim yourself a Catholic by education and conviction, and at the same time you permit the outrageous abuses that are being committed by the security forces in a country which we say is civilized and Christian." After expressing disgust at being refused entrance into Aguilares, he demanded a response to this question: "Can it be that even the person of the archbishop is seen as a danger to national security?" Romero already knew the answer. But he wanted Molina to say it publicly.[12] He'd come a long way from the diffident protest he'd made to Molina after the Tres Calles massacre two years earlier.

Operation Rutilio lasted for an entire month. During that time, no one was allowed to enter or leave the cordoned-off town. When the army finally departed on June 19, Romero immediately went to Aguilares to rededicate the defiled church, introduce a new pastoral team to the traumatized residents, and proclaim by word and deed his solidarity with them. At Mass, Romero told the huge crowd gathered in the church, "You are the image of the divine victim 'pierced for our offenses'... You are Christ today, suffering in history."[13] He then went on to say that innocent suffering, when borne with Christian fortitude and forgiveness, can serve as an inspiration to others and a rebuke to those who inflict it. Like Martin Luther King, Jr., Romero believed that the power of nonviolent resistance was its potential to afflict the consciences and waken the souls of oppressors. So, he urged, "Let there be no animosity in our heart.... Let us pray for the conversion of those who struck us [and] of those who sacrilegiously dared to lay hands on the sacred tabernacle."[14]

Afterward, the assembled people processed through the town square with Romero bringing up the rear holding a monstrance containing the consecrated Host. At one point the procession was halted by an armed phalanx of defiant guardsmen who clearly wanted to intimidate and break up the crowd. When Romero realized what was happening, he shouted *Adelante!*—"Let us go forward!"—and the people pushed past the soldiers. "From that day on," recalled theologian Jon Sobrino, "when any important event occurred in El Salvador, whether you were with him or against him, you always had to look to Monseñor Romero."[15]

But thus far, contrary to Romero's hope, consciences weren't being afflicted nor hearts converted. Instead, a dark perversion of Dom Hélder Câmara's spiral of violence had set in. Whenever *campesinos* and others nonviolently protested atrocities committed by the national guard, the military, or clandestine right-wing groups, the response was an acceleration of government-sanctioned violence. It was as if the example of nonviolence unleashed a demonic fury in the ruling elite.

This pattern was demonstrated the very day after the Aguilares processional. In retaliation for Romero's homiletic condemnation of what the national guard had done to the town and its people, the White Warriors Union issued an ultimatum: All Jesuit priests stationed in El Salvador had to leave the country or risk assassination. They had thirty days to decide. After that, the killing would begin.

Had the situation in El Salvador been less fraught, the sheer melodrama of the threat would have made it risible. But the White Warriors Union had claimed responsibility for the brutal murder of Fr. Alfonso Navarro just a few weeks earlier, and the Jesuit-operated Central American University had been bombed by right-wing groups no fewer than six times in the past year and a half. So Romero and the Jesuits took the ultimatum very seriously indeed. At the same time, however, they refused to be intimidated. The Jesuits immediately announced that they weren't going anywhere, Pedro Arrupe praised their courageous willingness to risk martyrdom, and domestic and international denunciations of the threat began flooding President Molina's office. For once, most likely because he felt the world's disapproving gaze upon him, Molina did the right thing. He ordered police protection for the Jesuits and issued a statement condemning the White Warrior Union's murderous threat. Thankfully, the late July deadline passed with no attack on the Jesuits. Either the threat had been sheer bluff, or officials who previously had turned a blind eye to the Union's atrocities warned them off seeing this one through.

By the time the deadline arrived, Molina was no longer president. The reins of power changed hands on July 1 with the inauguration of General Carlos Umberto Romero. Consistent with his announced intention to boycott official government events as long as Grande's murder went uninvestigated, Romero refused to attend. Once again, papal nuncio Gerada was furious with him, as were Bishops Alvarez and Barrera. All three of them attended the inauguration as guests of honor. But the archbishop's absence was palpable and its significance apparent to both his supporters and detractors. In a radio interview a few days later, Romero explained that he had no desire to break ties with the government. But he pointed out that genuine dialogue must be based on an affirmation of the importance of peace with justice, and that the government's policy of armed response to dissidents was a long way from that.

Peace with justice within the concrete context of El Salvador was uppermost in Romero's mind in the drafting of his second pastoral letter, released on Transfiguration Sunday, August 6, 1977. The Transfiguration, or Feast of the Divine Savior of the World as it's known in El Salvador, is an important day for Salvadoran Catholics, honoring as it does the nation's patron. That's why Romero chose the date as the occasion to release this pastoral letter, "The Church, the Body of Christ in History," as well as his final two letters in 1978 and 1979.

Jon Sobrino collaborated with Romero in the writing of the letter. The two of them drew heavily upon the teachings of Vatican II, Medellín, and *Evangelii Nuntiandi* to defend the thesis that the Church is the Body of Christ in history and as such is called to respond to the concrete exigencies of history. This means that the Church is always on the move, constantly adapting how it represents Christ to the world and how it interprets its responsibilities to the people it serves. "To remain anchored in a nonevolving traditionalism," wrote Romero, "whether out of ignorance or selfishness, is to close one's eyes to what is meant by authentic Christian tradition." Echoing a sentiment expressed by John XXIII when he called for the Vatican II Council, Romero insisted that the Church "is not a museum of souvenirs to be protected."[16]

An important new realization on the part of the Latin American Church, thanks to the bishops at Medellín, was that sin isn't simply a private act committed by an individual. It can also be institutionalized violence occurring "when there really is present a situation of permanent, structured injustice."[17] In such situations, the Church's obligation is to denounce the injustice, but to do so in a spirit of love rather than hatred or resentment. The ultimate goal, stressed Romero, isn't so much to condemn as to convert. The Church at its best embodies Christ's loving desire to "make all men and women truly human," both those who have "become dehumanized because of their desire for profits," and those who have been dehumanized "because pushed to the margins of society."[18] This is what distinguishes the Church's approach to human liberation from Marxist class warfare or guerrilla resistance.

Romero also emphasized that the Church "does not engage in party politics." But this doesn't negate the Church's obligation to speak truth to power. Quoting the Vatican II document *Gaudium et Spes*, Romero affirmed that "at all times and in all places, the Church should have true freedom to preach the faith, to teach its social doctrine, to exercise its role freely among humans, and also to pass moral judgment on those matters which regard public order when the fundamental rights of a person or the salvation of souls require it."[19]

To make sure that Salvadoran readers of his letter, especially those belonging to the political and economic elite, didn't miss his point about the historical embodiment of the Church, Romero pointed out that Christian hope in El Salvador "is linked inseparably with social justice, with a real improvement in the lot of [its] people, and especially an improvement in the lot of the impoverished, landless masses, [and] with defense of their human rights."[20] As if this wasn't enough to anger defenders of the status quo, Romero offered specific recommendations for alleviating the institutionalized violence rocking the nation. Expelled clergy should be allowed to return, the fate of *desaparecidos* must be revealed, arbitrary arrests had to cease, and due process had to be guaranteed. These reforms would help to "bring about sincere cooperation between government and church so as to create a just social order, one that would gradually eliminate unjust structures."[21]

Romero's second pastoral letter was an extraordinary testament to just how far he had traveled from his dark years in San Salvador when he considered the Jesuits and liberation theologians to be enemies of *la Iglesia*. He finally had shed the more straitjacketing effects of *romanità*. This didn't mean that he was any less devoted to the traditional roles of priestly ministry or to the goal of *salvación integral*, the redemption of body and soul. But he now had a broader and richer understanding of what it meant for the Church to be Church and for its members to live their faith in the reality of concrete situations. This vision would sustain him through the dangerous months ahead.

Three days after the pastoral letter's release, President Romero invited Archbishop Romero for a sit-down at the Presidential House. The president, who had served as Molina's minister of defense and given the green light to more than one military atrocity against "subversives," wanted to defuse accusations that the government was implicated in human rights abuses.

Romero agreed to meet with him but came armed with a three-point memo that mirrored the recommendations in his pastoral letter. The government had to account for the disappeared, free prisoners deprived of due process, and stop unwarranted arrests. This was to be done immediately. Next, steps had to be taken to improve the living conditions of *campesinos*. Finally, structural reform of the nation's political and economic institutions had to be undertaken to ensure a fairer distribution of the nation's wealth.

The president made some vague assurances but did nothing, even after the archbishop reminded him in a mid-September letter of the points they'd discussed. But Romero wasn't discouraged. In that same month he said in a homily, "Let us not tire of preaching love. Though we see the waves of violence succeed in drowning the fire of Christian love, love must win out; it is the only thing that can."[22]

Yet the killings continued. The day after his homiletic assurance that love would be victorious, three base community leaders from the village of El Salitre were rounded up by the national guard and brutally murdered with machetes. Romero traveled to the village to console the grieving survivors, afterward condemning the killings from the cathedral pulpit.

November turned out to be a particularly violent month. In the eastern Salvadoran town of Osicala, government troops clashed with locals. After killing a few of them, the soldiers descended on the rectory of the parish priest, Fr. Miguel Ventura, and arrested him and his sacristan. Over the next few hours, both men were interrogated and tortured. At one point, Ventura's arms were tied behind his back and he was hoisted by a rope attached to his wrists, nearly ripping his shoulders from their sockets. The justification for the abuse was that he and his sacristan were suspected of hiding weapons and Marxist literature. When Ventura's bishop, the military vicar of El Salvador and a staunch supporter of the national guard, heard of his priest's treatment, he casually remarked that Ventura got what was coming to him. He was tortured, Bishop Alvarez said, "as a man, not as a priest."[23] Romero, on the other hand, was furious and immediately excommunicated those responsible for torturing the priest and sacristan.

A friend who visited the jailed Ventura was also arrested by the national guard. He too was tortured for two weeks with electric shock and multiple punctures from an ice pick to force him to give up the names of "subversive" priests. When he was finally released, he reported his treatment to Romero and despairingly asked, "How long will this last, Monseñor? They're trying to rein us in by torturing us." Romero replied that he didn't have an answer, but warned that "putting ourselves on the side of the poor is going to mean a lot of bloodshed for us."[24]

In mid-November, in the midst of a factory workers strike, a Salvadoran businessman was killed while resisting a kidnapping attempt from one of the left-wing guerrilla groups that were cropping up all over the country. Romero held his funeral Mass in the cathedral, but the service was interrupted by government rowdies who shouted anti-Church slogans through bullhorns. One of the catcalls, *Sacerdotes de Belcebú, vayan todos a Moscú!*—"Priests of Beelzebub, go back to Moscow!"—was cheered by many of those in attendance. The very next day, Justo Mejía, a delegate of the Word and union organizer, was arrested by the national guard. When his body was discovered, even Salvadorans who were becoming desensitized to violence were horrified. Mejía's body was cut to ribbons. His eyes had been gouged out, and his corpse decapitated. The sheer savagery of his torture and murder was a breathtaking reminder of the moral deterioration occurring in El Salvador.

Instead of acting to halt the atrocities, President Romero's government doubled down later that month by issuing a "Law for Defense of Public Order." It criminalized criticism of the military, government, and existing social institutions, and legitimized the indefinite detention of any and all persons suspected of subversive activity. Romero publicly blasted the law three days after it was announced. Citing Thomas Aquinas, he warned that "a real law must be just and must be for society's common good. Otherwise it does not require obedience."[25] His implication, clear to the thousands of Salvadorans who heard his words on their radios, was that the law was unjust and could be morally resisted. In other words, the leader of the El Salvador Church was publicly recommending civil disobedience.

Romero's first year as archbishop of San Salvador was fraught with tragedy and bloodshed. Beginning with the murder of his friend Rutilio Grande, the violence continued ceaselessly through the succeeding months. It's no surprise that Romero, despite discovering a deep sense of purpose and solidarity in his pastoral role as the nation's most outspoken Catholic defender of civil rights and human dignity, felt the need for emotional and spiritual support from others. As he wrote in a December letter to a well-wisher, "Pray much for our archdiocese and for me so that the Lord will give us the grace to be faithful to the mission He has given us. It's a very difficult mission, especially when the church tries to make itself heard in a society where social sin is the norm."[26]

CHAPTER EIGHT

Romero Against the Bishops

"I was subjected to many false accusations by other bishops."[1]

Violent clashes among government forces, clandestine right-wing groups, and leftist rebels—confrontations in which innocent *campesinos* all too often were caught in the crossfire—continued throughout Romero's second year as archbishop. Particularly notable was a week of bloodshed at Easter, tragic in itself but also unfortunate because it fueled what was settling into a concerted campaign against Romero by the Salvadoran bishops and curial bureaucrats in Rome. Resisting it took up much of his time and energy in 1978.

Romero had been in the Church long enough to know that its traditional top-down hierarchical structure easily bred resentful jealousy on the part of subordinates. He also knew that such feelings could be especially intense among those already enjoying high ecclesial positions. But he was still dismayed by the intensity of the opposition, much of it downright spiteful, that he received from both his own bishops and Rome. It's the great irony of Romero's life that a man as imbued with the spirit of *romanità* as he was should have endured such harsh ecclesial disapproval.

The curia's campaign was sparked when Georgetown University announced at the beginning of the year that it intended to bestow

---

an honorary doctor of humanities degree upon Romero. Due largely to the crackdown on Jesuits in El Salvador before and after the murder of Rutilio Grande, Georgetown and the Central American University, both Jesuit institutions, had established close ties with each other. Georgetown officials intended the conferral of the degree as a sign of respect for Romero's courageous leadership and of solidarity with Jesuits working in Romero's troubled nation.

As a pro forma courtesy, Georgetown administrators informed Archbishop Jean Jadot, the apostolic delegate to Washington, DC, of their plans. Jadot in turn reported the news to his superiors in Rome. They apparently raised a red flag, because Jadot soon phoned the president of Georgetown to ask that the university withhold the degree lest its conferral exacerbate political tensions in El Salvador. At the same time, the prefect of the Congregation for Catholic Education put pressure on Jesuit Superior General Pedro Arrupe to withdraw the award. Neither Georgetown nor Arrupe backed down.

It's clear from the behind-the-scenes maneuvering that a few highly placed officials in the Church hierarchy were already dissatisfied with Romero's behavior as archbishop. Negative reports from papal nuncio Gerada and others about his feud with the government and his support of priests who worked with base communities were having an effect.

As a sign of deep respect for Romero, and perhaps as a token of defiance to the Vatican officials who tried to block the honorary doctorate, Georgetown officials made the unusual decision to travel to San Salvador to confer the degree rather than having the archbishop come to the United States to receive it. The ceremony took place in mid-February in the city's cathedral, jam-packed for the occasion.

In his acceptance speech, Romero noted the appropriateness of receiving the academic recognition in his cathedral, saying "I am the pastor and teacher of the faith in this archdiocese"—a pointed observation surely directed at critics who accused him of spreading false doctrine.[2] He went on to say that the degree represented recognition of "that noble cause of Christian humanism that our church proclaims and defends," a humanism proclaimed by both Vatican II and Medellín.[3] Reverting to one of the points he'd made in his second pastoral letter, Romero said that this humanism, which seeks to affirm the dignity of all human beings, isn't an abstract philosophy. Rather, "it starts from the situation in this world where there exists the duty of planting the kingdom of God now." Part of the duty is recognizing and calling out the institutional structures of sin that obstruct the kingdom.[4]

Romero then went out of his way to say that Georgetown's recognition properly belonged to his many collaborators in the cause of justice, not only Roman Catholic laypersons and priests but also Protestants and even those who had no religious allegiance. It was a remarkable tribute from a man who just a few years earlier had viewed Salvadoran Protestants as heretics to be avoided.

Rising to a level of eloquence that kept his audience spellbound and prompted several interruptions of spontaneous applause, Romero concluded by saying that he saw the bestowal of the degree as a sign of hope that the world beyond El Salvador's borders was in solidarity with "the tragic experience of those who have been abused, those whom the church has believed it its duty to defend, and to denounce the abuses. This voice raised in defense and denunciation has too often been silenced, distorted, or calumniated by those with vested interests, or naively misunderstood by some at home and abroad." Georgetown's honorary degree showed that "honor, respect, and admiration is being shown to the sufferings, the fear, insecurity, and marginalization endured by so many of my brothers and sisters. This fact is a ray of comfort."[5]

Romero would shortly need the boost in morale given him by Georgetown's recognition. Just one month later, during Holy Week and Easter Week, violence broke out in a particularly ugly way.

On March 19, Palm Sunday, national guardsmen roared into the town of San Pedro Perulapán, located just a few miles outside of San Salvador. The government ordered them there ostensibly to quell unionized *campesinos* who supposedly were terrorizing the town's residents. An archdiocesan investigation later concluded that this was a bogus accusation and that the real reason for the operation was to intimidate critics of the ruling regime.

Throughout the next few days, guardsmen and ORDEN members rampaged through the town and surrounding countryside burning houses and beating *campesinos*. They also kidnapped, murdered, and mutilated a union leader, leaving his headless corpse in plain view as a warning.

The situation became so perilous that refugees from the violence fled to San Salvador and took refuge within the buildings of San José de la Montaña seminary, where they remained until the middle of April. Meanwhile, Romero and Bishop Marco Revelo, his vicar general, did their best to ease tensions, including negotiating for a guarantee of safety for members of the Popular Revolutionary Bloc who had taken refuge in the cathedral. Revelo's collaboration with the archbishop during this crisis would make his future opposition to Romero, soon to be on full display, particularly disheartening.

Offering sanctuary to the refugees in the seminary was the occasion for Romero's conservative fellow bishops, especially Aparicio, to go after him. Aparicio, who happened to be serving at the time as president of CEDES, the Salvadoran bishops' conference, had taken an intense personal dislike to Romero and went out of his way to obstruct him whenever possible.

In Romero's first year as archbishop, Aparicio had called for shutting down the seminary, which had resumed educating men for the priesthood after shutting its doors in the early 1970s, on the grounds that instructors were indoctrinating students with Communist propaganda. When his efforts met with no success, he decided to attack on a different front: He targeted the diocesan administrative offices, which were housed in one of the seminary buildings. Aparicio wanted them gone. His pretext was that the close proximity of seminary and diocesan offices made for interoffice confusion. But his real purpose was to undermine what he saw as Romero's episcopal support of leftist professors who were contaminating the minds of seminarians with liberation theology—and to be as much of a nuisance as possible to Romero.

In response, Romero and his aides did some tidying up of administrative boundaries that separated seminary and diocesan budgets and activities. But that wasn't good enough for Aparicio, who filed an official complaint with the Holy See asking Rome to order the removal of diocesan headquarters from the seminary building—a particularly arrogant move, given that the archdiocese actually owned the property. The Holy See complied, instructing Romero through Gerada to clear out of the seminary building so that activities such as hospitality to political refugees wouldn't interfere with priestly formation. (One might have thought that the opportunity to minister to refugees would've been a valuable bonus for the formation program.) The order, an obvious rebuke to Romero, delighted both Aparicio and the nuncio.

Simultaneous with this challenge to the archbishop's authority was an even more troublesome imbroglio sparked by a letter of protest sent in early March to Gerada. The letter was signed by nearly three hundred of the eleven hundred priests, nuns, and religious serving in El Salvador. They'd taken notice of the papal nuncio's cozy relationship with the nation's political and economic ruling class, his dislike of Romero, and his staunch opposition to Medellín's insistence that the Church's mission included addressing the social injustices that blight body and soul. They decided to call him out.

Their letter pulled no punches. Saying that they felt a "grave pastoral obligation" to speak some unpleasant truths to the nuncio about his obstructionist public and private machinations, the signers warned that his actions created "grave scandal for the people of God and are destructive for the Church and its evangelizing mission."[6]

Gerada's objectionable acts were then enumerated: collaboration with the perpetrators of repression, undermining the authority of the archbishop, and being insensitive to "the silent sorrow of the oppressed and persecuted peasantry, to the tears of the widows and mothers of the disappeared...and to our people's hunger for bread and for truth." The letter concluded with a fervent prayer that Gerada would repent and renounce his subservience to "Caiaphas, Herod, and Pilate."[7]

Gerada hit the roof when he received the letter, seeing it as not only hideously insubordinate but more evidence of how Romero was doing nothing to rein in the subversives among his clergy. He immediately forwarded the letter to the bishops' conference.

It was on the top of the agenda at their next gathering scheduled for March 15.

The meeting was tumultuous. Bishop Aparicio, hostile as usual, came out swinging by proclaiming that he intended to suspend the ten priests from his diocese who had signed the letter. Bishop Alvarez insisted that Romero was behind the letter, in spirit if not in deed, because of his tolerance of priests who polluted religion with politics. Romero denied having a hand in the letter—its language, he said, was too disrespectful for his taste—but he and Bishop Rivera argued that the grievances outlined in it deserved to be examined and discussed. Its signatories ought not to be punished for forthrightly expressing concerns, even if their language was intemperate.

Romero wrote to Gerada—his choice to do so rather than meeting him face-to-face reveals just how badly relations between the two had deteriorated—to assure the nuncio that he had no hand in drafting the letter of protest. But Gerada, like Bishops Aparacio, Alvarez, Barrera, and Revelo, nonetheless held him responsible.

All this might have remained a behind-church-doors spat but for the bishops' dislike of Romero, whom they blamed for upsetting the Salvadoran Church's amiable relations with the ruling class. When copies of the letter to Gerada were leaked to Mexican and Guatemalan newspapers, as well as one in San Salvador, they decided to respond publicly. The bishops drafted a statement and convened an emergency meeting on April 3 to rubberstamp it. Because Bishop Rivera was out of town and unable to attend, Romero was left to face the fire-breathing bishops without his one and only episcopal ally. The vote was four to one in favor of publishing the response.

In their statement, the bishops expressed outrage at what they saw as the insolence of Gerada's critics, charging them with assuming for themselves the authority to censure the pope's representative. This was pretty much boilerplate indignation which still might not have attracted a great deal of public attention. But then the bishops made a tactical error. They decided that they needed to enumerate in detail all the original letter's charges against Gerada to show how ridiculous they believed them to be. When the statement was published two days later, the cat was out of the bag, and the entire nation was apprised, via the very bishops who supported him and opposed Romero, of Gerada's malfeasances. The list, and not the bishop's objections, became the focus of attention.

The bishops' initial mid-March meeting to discuss the letter to the nuncio had been acrimonious enough. But at the second one when they approved their public response to it, their attacks on the archbishop were so brutal as to seem at times nearly unhinged. They wounded Romero so deeply that he felt the need to ruminate on them in two separate diary entries.

He had been subjected, he noted in a painfully understated way, "to many false accusations."[8] His preaching was divisive; his priests agitators of *campesino* revolt; his archdiocese in chaos; and the presence of his headquarters in the seminary—that complaint again!—a toxic influence on the curriculum.

Nor did the recrimination end there. Aparicio specifically accused Romero of undercutting the authority of the bishops in their own dioceses; Alvarez "took the opportunity to voice his disagreement with me," and Barrera "called my preaching violent." But the cruelest jab was the betrayal of his vicar general Revelo, the same man who just days before had worked with Romero to negotiate safe passage for unionists barricaded in the cathedral. He archly informed the archbishop that he "was not infallible" in interpreting Church teaching on social justice, and "that, therefore, [Revelo] was not obliged to agree with [Romero's] approach."[9]

The hubbub over the letter to Gerada barely had time to calm down before the archbishop was embroiled in another assault on his moral character and ecclesial authority. In a homily delivered at the end of April, he had criticized Salvadoran judges, including even those who served on the nation's highest court, for turning blind eyes to extrajudicial abuses like the torture of prisoners. He spoke of "judges that sell themselves" to the nation's political and economic elite and who thereby mock both democracy and the rule of law.

A week later, the supreme court published a letter in the press demanding that Romero back up his claim about "venal judges" (a term Romero hadn't used) by disclosing their names. The Salvadoran judiciary had now joined the bishops' efforts to discredit Romero.

In his Pentecost homily delivered in mid-May, Romero stood by his original statement. Since the supreme court had chosen to engage him in public debate instead of a civil lawsuit, he told his congregation that he felt under no obligation to reveal names. The insinuation, lost on no one, was that the identities of corrupt judges were already well known to the public. Instead, he hammered away at the supreme court's "absolute contempt" for the law in its disregard of habeas corpus and willingness to sanction arbitrary arrests that ran roughshod over due process. He accused the supreme court of systematically violating both the Salvadoran constitution and the United Nation's Universal Declaration of Human Rights.

Romero wanted everyone listening to his words to be clear on one point: His charge against El Salvador's judges wasn't based on a "malicious desire to defame," but on his recognition that "as a pastor of a people suffering injustice" he had a duty to speak out on their behalf when the law refused to protect them. In doing so, said Romero, "I am ready to face trial and prison, even though they would only add another injustice" to the long list of those already plaguing El Salvador.[10]

Romero's homily was greeted with enthusiasm from people throughout the nation. Its popularity convinced the supreme court, doubtlessly after consulting with the government, that it would be imprudent to pursue the matter further.

Given the trouble that Romero was having with the bishops, nuncio, and secular authorities, he guessed that wildly unfavorable reports about him were making their way to Rome. His hunch was proven right in May when he received a frosty letter from Cardinal Sebastiano Baggio, prefect of the Sacred Congregation for the Bishops, inviting him to the Vatican to respond to the complaints. Accompanied by Bishop Rivera and Fr. Ricardo Urioste, who shared vicar general duties with Bishop Revelo, Romero arrived in the Eternal City in mid-June feeling somewhat like an errant schoolboy hauled up before the headmaster. But he also was determined, as he wrote in his diary, to lay before Baggio "all the interests, concerns, problems, hopes, plans, and afflictions of all my priests, religious communities, parishes, and grass-roots communities."[11]

His meeting with Baggio a couple of days later was demoralizing. The cardinal obviously put a lot of stock in the negative reports about Romero. He accused him of allowing himself to be coopted by leftist elements in El Salvador, of refusing to cultivate collegiality with his brother bishops, and of being complicit in the letter of protest to Gerada. He even criticized the length of his homilies, although he admitted, somewhat reluctantly, that they contained no doctrinal errors. Romero responded that in his episcopal ministry he was simply following the spirit of the Gospel and the letter of Vatican II and Medellín, that the absence of collegiality with the Salvadoran bishops was because they undermined trust, the basis of collegiality, that he'd had no foreknowledge of the Gerada letter, and that his homilies, despite being lengthy, kept the attention of the faithful.

The day after this dressing-down by Baggio, Romero was thumped again, this time by Cardinal Gabriel-Marie Garrone, prefect of the Congregation for Catholic Education, the same official who back in February had tried to quash Georgetown's bestowal of a degree on Romero. The cardinal said he had received reports that the San José de la Montaña seminary was drilling future priests in Marxist ideology. Romero denied the charge, telling Garrone that he so respected the faculty's commitment to the Gospels and loyalty to the Church that he would never question their integrity or dedication.

Romero stood his ground in these two interviews, although it is unclear how successful he was in convincing either Baggio or Garrone that the unfavorable reports about him were false. So even though he was excited about his and Rivera's next appointment, a special audience with Pope Paul VI, he also went into it a bit deflated. Romero remembered how a year earlier Paul had taken him by the hands and reminded him that he was the man in charge of El Salvador's Roman Catholic community. He hoped to receive a similar vote of confidence this time around.

And he did. Paul once again warmly grasped Romero's hands and spoke exactly the words the beleaguered archbishop needed to hear. Romero quoted them later that day in his diary. "I understand your difficult work," the pope said. "It is a work that can be misunderstood; it requires a great deal of patience and a great deal of strength. I already know that not everyone thinks like you do.... Nevertheless, proceed with courage, with patience, with strength, with hope."[12]

Just as important as this expression of confidence in Romero the man was the pope's obvious heartfelt sympathy for the plight of the Salvadoran *campesinos*. Paul said that he knew "they were a generous, hard-working people and that today they suffer a great deal and demand their rights." He urged Romero "to help them, work on their behalf, but never with hatred [or by] fomenting violence, rather basing [his] actions on great love." The pope recognized that Romero was up against the nation's "dominant powers," but that only the power of love could wear down their resistance.[13]

Romero was incredibly heartened by his meeting with Paul. "The pope," he confided to his diary, is "the true father of all.... I have felt him so near to me, I leave feeling so grateful to him, that my heart, my faith, my spirit continue to draw nourishment from that rock where the church's unity is so palpable."[14]

On his return to El Salvador, Romero set to work on his third pastoral letter, collaborating this time with Bishop Rivera. The three topics he explored in it were the Church's proper relationship to unions and popular political organizations, the ongoing personal and institutional violence embroiling the nation, and the accelerating accusations from Romero's critics that he was mingling religion and politics and thereby encouraging the violence. In his letter, he wanted to analyze the first and respond to the second and third.

Romero intended to release the letter on the Feast of the Transfiguration, exactly one year since his last one. Sadly, Pope Paul VI, who had been in declining health for some time, died on that very day. Circumstances delayed its publication, thereby allowing Romero the opportunity to add a heartfelt tribute to the late pontiff in the document's final version.

Romero asserted the duty of the Church Universal to call out and respond to injustice. It "would be wrong," he wrote, for the Church "to remain silent when faced with concrete problems."[15] He insisted that since many of those problems are caused by institutions that favor the wealthy at the expense of the poor, the poor have an obvious right, affirmed by Vatican II, Medellín, papal encyclicals, and the Universal Declaration of Human Rights, to resist the institutional threat to their political, economic, and personal well-being by unionizing and joining together in political organizations and base communities.

The Church's first and foremost mission is to evangelize the world. But when historical circumstances warrant it, the Church is also obliged to exert its moral authority to support the poor in their legitimate struggle for basic human rights. Even though the Church is not and should never be mistaken for a political entity, "it can and must pass judgment on the general intention and the particular methods of political parties and organizations, precisely because of its interest in a more just society." Such an activity "is not alien to the definitive liberation achieved in Jesus Christ."[16]

But the Church's involvement, as Pope Paul had emphasized in his final meeting with Romero, must always aim for "a conversion of heart and mind," not simply structural changes in government or society, and so necessarily rejects violence as "ineffective and out of keeping with the dignity of the people."[17] This principle led Romero to turn to an analysis of the different levels of violence, ranging from institutionalized varieties that wickedly serve the powerful against the weak to legitimate forms of proportional self-defense. He noted, in agreement with Medellín, that from a moral perspective, "the Christian can fight, but prefers peace to war." Nonviolence is a "constructive dynamism" that's anything but passive acquiescence to injustice. It's a powerful force capable of converting hearts and changing society.[18]

Genuine peace, the letter concludes, must be built upon justice. Otherwise, any cessation of hostilities is ephemeral. Justice in El Salvador will never be possible, and hence peace never sustainable, "as long as the powerful minority persists in its intransigence and refuses to accept even the smallest changes." The "most urgent task" for the Salvadoran Church, then, is cooperating with and supporting political organizations and unions that work nonviolently for a more equitable social system.[19]

Romero's third pastoral letter was welcomed by priests and laypersons working in base communities, by *campesinos* who heard summaries of it by word of mouth, and by unionists and dissidents throughout the whole of Latin America. But it also fanned the flames of rage in El Salvador's ruling elite as well as the bishops and papal nuncio who already labeled Romero a Communist dupe, or worse. For his part, Romero had ceased to care overly much what his fellow bishops thought of him. His blood was up and he refused to let them bully or intimidate him.

Romero's growing resolve was displayed when Cardinal Albino Luciani succeeded Pope Paul on August 26 and took the name

John Paul I. Gerada threw a celebratory bash at the nunciature and invited everybody who was anybody in San Salvador, including the archbishop, to attend. Romero declined, believing that his attendance would give the public the false impression that he was on cordial terms with the dignitaries who would be there.

This rebuff was the final straw for Gerada, who took Romero's absence as a personal snub. In his anger, he resolved to recommend that Rome remove Romero as archbishop. Romero, somehow getting wind of this, decided to preempt Gerada by writing personally to the pope defending himself. But by then, the first John Paul had died after just a month as pope, so Romero addressed his letter to John Paul II. It was dated October 17, exactly one day after John Paul II was elected.

What seemed a good idea at the time, and one that clearly reflected Romero's determination to do what he believed right regardless of the personal cost, was in retrospect probably a blunder. The new Polish-born pope had spent most of his adult life and all of his ministry under the brutalizing heel of Soviet-style Communism, and so had little patience with or understanding of the vast differences between Latin American liberation theology and Soviet-style socialism. To him, the southern Church's involvement in the struggle for justice smacked of Communist infiltration. By temperament and experience, therefore, he was inclined to accept at face value reports that accused Romero of flirting with, if not actually embracing, Communist ideology.

So Romero's epistolary effort to justify his stand, as he put it, "at the side of my oppressed and abused people" was a bit suspect from the very start. His harsh words about the papal nuncio and Salvadoran bishops didn't help his case either. For anyone without a full knowledge of the bishops' war against him, his criticisms of them come across as churlish and exaggerated, especially to a pontiff like John Paul who valued Church discipline and proper observance of protocol. Romero described Gerada in terms that made him seem like a capitalist flunkey. Alvarez was dismissed as a poor pastor and Barrera an old man who never had much "evangelical commitment to his people." Romero's resentment of Revelo's betrayal prompted a fervent request that he be transferred to another diocese.

But his most brutal evaluation was reserved for Bishop Aparicio. Romero's words quiver with anger and resentment in his description of his chief rival as "supremely fickle, vain, and self-seeking." He was also, continued Romero, a weathercock who opposed or defended the government and Church as his own self-interest dictated, and his behavior as president of the bishops' conference had been "arbitrary and very disloyal."[20]

In all fairness, part of Romero's angry denunciation of Aparicio may have been prompted by a remark the bishop had made two days before the archbishop sat down to write his letter to the new pope. The national guard had arrested two of Aparicio's priests on charges of subversion. Instead of standing up for them, Aparicio sided with the authorities—which, Romero concluded, was both a personally dishonorable move and a precedent-setting one that "could be dangerous for the archdiocese."[21]

The bishops would resume their frontal attack the following year, Romero's last full one as archbishop. Early in May 1979, Revelo, Alvarez, Aparicio, and Barrera dispatched a ten-page document to Rome in which they assailed Romero in language that was extreme even for them. They bizarrely accused slain priests Rutilio Grande and Alfonso Navarra of being secret leftists killed by their Communist associates rather than by national guardsmen or right-wing death squads. Romero was a leftist agitator who incited class warfare in his homilies. He regularly undermined the authority of the magisterium and, even worse, "manipulates the Bible, adulterates the figure of Jesus Christ our Lord, portraying him as a subversive, a revolutionary, and a political leader."[22] The bishops' charges against Romero are so out of touch with reality that one wonders if they actually believed them, or if they hated him so much that they were willing to perjure themselves to do him harm. Perhaps a bit of both.

Two welcome events in the midst of Romero's yearlong battles with ecclesial and secular authorities occurred in late November. First, he discovered that a sizeable group of British parliamentarians, impressed with his advocacy for El Salvador's poor, had nominated him for a Nobel Peace Prize. Their endorsement was soon seconded by a number of American congresspersons.

Second, Bishop Marco Revelo finally overstepped his authority in such an egregious way that Romero was justified in dismissing him as his vicar general. Without consulting Romero, he simply signed over the archbishop's legal leadership of the Catholic charity Caritas to none other than Bishop Aparicio. It came out later that he had done so with the encouragement and support of President Romero's government, yet another indication that the archbishop was a thorn in the side of state as well as Church. But it was enough to rid Romero of Revelo, and for that the archbishop must have breathed a sigh of relief.

But then, all hell broke out. Two more of Romero's priests were murdered.

CHAPTER NINE

Voice of the Voiceless

"If we want to be a church that responds to the people's sufferings, we must make our own these cries."[1]

As 1978 was drawing to a close, Romero received word that Fr. Ernesto "Neto" Barerra had been killed. He died on November 28 in a gunfight with national guardsmen. But the difference this time was that the Popular Liberation Forces (FPL) claimed him as one of their own. They issued a public statement extolling him as a "revolutionary combatant" who had died valiantly with weapons in his hands.

While it is true that Barrera's ministry had focused on establishing base communities and *campesino* unions, it is unclear whether he actually had taken up arms with leftist guerrillas or if the FPL was manipulating the news of his death for propaganda purposes. What is beyond question, however, is that he was tortured before he died; his body was covered with cigarette burns, an interrogation technique favored by security forces.

Romero was unsure how to respond to the death. He'd never wavered in his opposition to violence, especially when advocated or indulged in by clergy. Yet Barrera had been one of his priests. If he refused to preside at his funeral, he would appear as cold-hearted as Aparicio had been when his own diocesan priests were tortured. But if he did preside, given the rumors of Barrera's membership in the FPL, it might look as if he endorsed violence. Ultimately, Romero decided that as bishop he was Barrera's spiritual father and owed him the paternal respect and care that any father would show a dead son. "We're going to say goodbye to him with a Mass," he told some of his associates, "like the priest that he is."[2]

The death of another priest, Octavio Ortiz, followed just a few weeks later. This one hit Romero particularly hard because he'd ordained Ortiz. On January 20, during a retreat Fr. Ortiz was conducting for thirty teenagers at a center called El Despertar ("The Awakening"), the national guard struck. Breaking through the gate of the retreat center with a tank, soldiers began firing indiscriminately on everyone they saw. Four youngsters were riddled with bullets. Ortiz, to the shouts of "Kill him! Crush him!", was shot and then flattened by the tank. Afterward, the bodies of the teenagers were placed on El Despertar's roof with pistols in their hands to make them look like combatants. Almost immediately, the government issued reports insisting that the retreat center had been targeted by the military because it was actually a school for guerrillas.

The night before he was killed, Ortiz and the teenagers had been discussing two questions inspired by their reading of the Gospels: "What does it mean to give sight to the blind? What does it mean to free the oppressed?" This was the "subversion" Ortiz was teaching. The two questions were later engraved on the slab covering his grave.

When Romero went to the morgue later that day, he was shocked by how unrecognizable Ortiz's body was. Breaking down at the horrific sight, he wept as he rocked the young priest's flattened corpse in his arms. When he left, his cassock was covered in blood.

At the funeral for Ortiz and the four other victims, Romero's anger came through unmistakably in his homily. President Romero had boasted to reporters while on a state visit to Mexico that there was no persecution of the Church in El Salvador. "But here in the cathedral, we see the proof that he is a liar!" thundered Romero. "A priest murdered by the national guard, and four young men killed with him.... They are the messengers of the reality of our people."[3] From this point until his own murder, Romero's denunciation of government oppression was increasingly uncompromising—and increasingly dangerous.

There was good reason for Romero stepping up his public condemnation of the government: *campesino* unionists, delegates of the word, and political activists were being arrested, disappeared, or murdered at a bewildering rate. In 1979 and 1980, an estimated three thousand people were killed or disappeared in El Salvador. In President Romero's first year in office, a full seven hundred deaths were recorded; the following year the body count nearly doubled. There was rarely a morning when mutilated and tortured corpses weren't discovered dumped in public squares or rubbish heaps as grisly warnings to others. No wonder Romero sadly remarked at one point, "It seems that my vocation is to go around picking up bodies."[4]

Nor was the violence exclusively the government's, although certainly the bulk of it was. The armed guerrilla groups springing up in the countryside were more than ready to retaliate by murdering, bombing, kidnapping, and rioting. Romero appealed to them as much as to the military to cease the violence. He even met several times with rebel leaders in the hope of persuading them that their tactics only contributed to the spiral of violence into which the nation was sinking. But his efforts were unsuccessful.

As he confided to his diary after one of the clandestine meetings, "these people are firmly convinced that it is not the force of love that will resolve the situation, but rather the force of violence. They do not want to listen to reason, much less hear about Christian love."[5]

The day after Ortiz's funeral, Romero left for the Latin American Bishops' Conference (CELAM) at Puebla, Mexico. Pope John Paul II flew in to open it, just as Paul VI had done for the one at Medellín a few years earlier. The conference would affirm Medellín's espousal of the preferential option for the poor as well as the Church's duty to appeal to the conscience of Latin America's ruling elites, even if that meant publicly defying them and encouraging resistance from the faithful.

Romero took a back seat at the conference, partly because he was by nature reserved in unfamiliar public settings but also because he was bothered by eye problems, perhaps a psychosomatic consequence of his shock at Ortiz's brutal murder. But he did give several press interviews in which he spoke frankly about the deteriorating situation in El Salvador and his belief that his ministry with *campesinos* had helped him discover his true vocation. As he said to one reporter, "To be converted is to return to the true God and, in this sense, I feel that my contact with the poor, with those in need, brings me to feel even more my need of God."[6]

Romero's interviews were wildly popular, making him a central figure at the conference despite his hanging back during the actual proceedings. President Romero sourly accused him of grandstanding. Bishop Aparacio, who was also at Puebla, tried hard to convince reporters that the archbishop was a Marxist who was ruining the Salvadoran Church. But his accusations convinced no one who didn't already have it in for Romero.

During the conference, Romero served on a committee charged with composing a statement about evangelization and human development in Latin America. His recommendations are in keeping with the vision outlined in his pastoral letters and preached in his Sunday homilies. Effective evangelization in the Latin American context, he wrote, is only possible if it calls out political injustice and economic inequality, denounces arbitrary arrest and torture, supports the right of *campesinos* to organize, and encourages priests to continue their work in building base communities. His efforts on the committee reflected his conviction, expressed in one of his Puebla interviews, that the Church was called upon to "echo" the "anguish" of the repressed. "If we want to be a church that responds to the people's sufferings, we must make our own these cries. If we do not, we are not giving all the response that God wants to give to those who suffer."[7]

Romero returned to El Salvador energized and heartened by the happy discovery that most of the Puebla attendees agreed with his, rather than Aparicio's, view of the Church's proper mission. But it was becoming alarmingly clear that the country was on the brink of civil war. The months of May and June proved to be especially bloody.

The first blow was what came to be called the "Tuesdays of May" crisis because several Tuesdays of the month brought new explosions of violence to the country, making May the deadliest single month in El Salvador since *la Matanza* in 1932.

The initial Tuesday outbreak of violence occurred on May 8, when demonstrators protesting the arrest of union leaders began occupying embassy buildings and churches in San Salvador and taking hostages. Their supporters clogged the streets, smashing store windows and chanting resistance slogans. Before long, national guardsmen and FPL guerrillas were openly battling one another throughout the city. The violence climaxed when government forces began firing into a large crowd assembled in front of the cathedral. Terrified protesters sought sanctuary in the cathedral, dragging their wounded in with them and leaving at least twenty-five corpses in the plaza. Security forces initially refused to let medical personnel attend to the wounded. But the arrival of television cameras and international journalists eventually caused them to back down. Horrified at the number of dead and injured, Romero publicly blasted both sides for the bloody confrontation. The bishops' conference remained silent.

The following Tuesday, national guardsmen attacked more protesters, this time on the outskirts of San Salvador. When reporters asked for his reaction, Romero frankly replied that things were getting out of control because "people are no longer willing to keep on enduring the deep structural crisis that the country is suffering."[8] That Sunday, still more demonstrations erupted in several towns, most of them in response to the first bloody Tuesday. Once again government forces brutally quelled them, killing or wounding nearly 150 participants.

On May 22, the third Tuesday of the month, a group of insurgents tried to break through a cordon the government had set up around the Venezuelan embassy. It was still occupied by FPL members who were running out of food and water, and their comrades assaulted the barricade to get badly needed supplies to them. Fourteen of them were killed and another sixteen wounded in the unsuccessful attempt. The next day the FPL retaliated by murdering the minister of education, whereupon the White

Warrior Union killed a couple of "subversives." Dom Hélder Câmara's spiral of violence had never been more obvious.

The month of June was even worse with the number of slain or disappeared, a full thirty of them teachers accused of poisoning the minds of students with Marxist propaganda, skyrocketing. Also victimized were labor leaders, *campesino* delegates of the Word, political dissidents, and anyone else the government perceived as a threat. The armed resistance groups, growing in number and daring as government-sponsored violence increased, responded with assassinations and bombings.

Then, toward the end of the month, another priest was killed. He was Rafael Palacios, who worked with base communities and had taken over the parish of the murdered Octavio Ortiz. He was the fifth priest slain since Romero was installed as archbishop. Men in an unmarked car accosted him on his way to his church and tried to force him to go with him. When he resisted, they shot him down and left him dying in the street.

Palacios had actually visited Romero just a few days earlier to tell him he had been threatened by the White Warrior Union. A member of the death squad had painted the Union's death sentence, a white hand, on his car. By this time, it had become commonplace for Salvadoran priests to receive threats. Romero himself got them on a regular basis. Additionally, the military was beginning to harass him at roadblocks, even demanding that he exit his car and submit to body searches. So Romero wasn't overly concerned about the threat to Palacios.

At Palacios's funeral, which Romero celebrated in the cathedral, Romero's anger at the murder—as well as, perhaps, remorse at not taking the threat against his priest's life more seriously—came through loud and clear. He condemned the "forces of hell and murder" that had killed Palacios and were terrorizing the entire country. The murder wasn't simply the act of two or three evil men but a symptom of the structural sin that El Salvador's repressive economic and political institutions fostered. Although he deeply regretted the violent death of any of his priests, Romero noted that it would be scandalously wrong if priests remained unharmed in a land where people from all walks of life were regularly butchered. That's because priests should be the living "testimony of a church incarnated in the problems of its people."[9]

In the midst of all this violence, Romero decided that another damage control visit to Rome was called for. Back in December 1978, he'd been shocked to discover that the Vatican had named Argentinian bishop Antonio Quarracino as apostolic visitor to Romero's archdiocese. On the face of things, this was an obvious sign of low confidence in Romero, if not outright distrust on the part of the curia. Apostolic visitors are troubleshooters sent to dioceses whose bishops are suspected of incompetence. Their job is to observe what's going on and report back to the Vatican. The very fact that Quarracino had been appointed, coupled with the relentless criticism of Romero coming from Salvadoran bishops, oligarchs, and politicians, convinced him that it was time for an audience with the pope.

Although Romero submitted a request for a private meeting with John Paul II well before his visit in early May, once in Rome he was blocked for several days by curial indifference and bureaucratic incompetence. Romero was hurt and troubled by what he perceived as a deliberate snub to his authority. "I am still very concerned about the attitude they show to the pastor of a diocese, considering that I asked for this audience some time ago," he confided to his diary. Nonetheless, he put himself "in God's hands.... I believe in and love the Holy Church and, with God's grace, I will always be faithful to the Holy See, to the teaching of the pope."[10] Romero's loyalty to the Church was unquestionably sincere. But his diary entry indicated that he anticipated his interview with the pope was going to be unpleasant.

The meeting finally occurred on May 7. Romero arrived with a thick file of documents on the situation in El Salvador and a photograph of Octavio Ortiz. (It will be remembered that in his first audience with Pope Paul VI, he had given the pontiff a photograph of the recently slain Rutilio Grande. Romero believed it was important to gaze upon the faces of martyrs lest they became anonymous statistics.) John Paul accepted the file and photograph, but put them to one side and, Romero recalled in his diary, began to lecture him on how difficult pastoral work is in a "political climate like the one in which I have to work. He recommended great balance and prudence, especially when denouncing specific situations." John Paul's insinuation was that in speaking out against government-sanctioned violence and repression, Romero hadn't been practicing balance and prudence. It was the same criticism he'd received from the prefect for the Congregation of Bishops on an earlier visit to Rome.

Then came the bombshell: The pope told Romero that apostolic visitor Quarracino had reported that the Church's situation in El Salvador was "an extremely delicate one," and recommended that "to resolve the deficiencies in pastoral work and the lack of harmony among the bishops, an apostolic administrator *sede plena* be appointed."[11] This was an unambiguous vote of no confidence in the archbishop, even though Quarracino apparently liked Romero personally, because an administrator *sede plena* becomes the person actually in charge of a diocese.

Had a *sede plena* administrator been appointed, Romero would have retained the title of archbishop but his authority would have been reduced to the merely ceremonial. In effect, he would have been hung out to dry and his public criticisms of the government censored if not halted. To his credit, John Paul refrained from acting on Quarracino's recommendation right away, and Romero's murder less than a year later made the point moot. But the very fact that the pope mentioned the recommendation to Romero during the audience was a clear warning: Put your house in order.

In recording his own understated response to the meeting, Romero merely said that he left it "not feel[ing] completely satisfied," and stoically observed, "I have learned that one cannot expect always to get complete approval and that it is more useful to hear criticism that can be used to improve our work."[12] His entry may have been as passionless as it was because he was trying to honor his earlier diary resolution to show loyalty to Church and pope. But an acquaintance to whom Romero described the meeting a few days later remembered that he was so upset by it that he was "practically in tears." According to her, Romero confessed that the pope coldly scolded him for not cultivating better relations with the Salvadoran government. But what upset Romero the most was what he perceived as John Paul's skepticism about Romero's assurance that the murdered Fr. Ortiz hadn't been a Communist agitator. It was obvious that other voices had already gotten to John Paul.[13]

Interestingly, despite the escalating national turmoil and his uneasy relationship with the Vatican, Romero began to experience during these months a peace of mind and even spiritual joy that had eluded him most of his adult life, plagued as he'd always been by scrupulosity and a naturally anxious temperament. He attributed the new calm to his growing conviction that in serving the poor, he was doing exactly what God wanted from him. As he told a reporter at Puebla, his ministry to them offered him the gift of genuine conversion.

Although by this time his defiance of the government and defense of the poor had made him something of an international celebrity, Romero continued to live in the same modest way he always had. When he became archbishop he declined to use the official episcopal residence, instead asking the nuns who ran Divine Providence Hospital, a care facility for patients dying of cancer, if he could live on their grounds. As bishop of Santiago de María, he had always stayed with them on visits to San Salvador, sleeping in a small room off the sacristy. The sisters gladly agreed to the new archbishop's request and even built him a tiny bungalow on the hospital grounds where he lived for the rest of his life. He rarely invited visitors to the house—it was his refuge from the cares of office—but gladly took his meals with the sisters in their dining room.

Although he obviously had administrative duties, Romero was first and foremost a pastoral archbishop, conscientious in visiting parishes to offer comfort and hope to anyone who had suffered, directly or indirectly, from the repression and violence that had become the norm in El Salvador. He encouraged a handful of idealistic and courageous young lawyers to establish a Legal Aid Office to represent people unable to pay for attorney services, investigate government-sponsored violence against dissidents, and uncover information about the fate of the swelling number of *desaparecidos*. Romero's door was always open to grieving family members who came to him from all parts of the country to ask for help in finding their missing loved ones. He would listen to them for hours and was especially solicitous of distraught mothers. In one of his homilies, he compared their suffering to that of Mary as she stood at the foot of the Cross.

On August 4, Alirio Napoleón Macías became the sixth priest to die at the hands of a death squad. The week before, newspapers had published information he had given them about raids and killings in his parish, and they had rashly named him as their source. This made him a marked man. The three thugs sent to murder him found him in his church, shot him multiple times, and left him dead next to the altar. Macías was a priest in Bishop Aparicio's diocese. For once, the ultra-conservative enemy of Romero actually criticized the government, calling for an investigation into his priest's murder and excommunicating his killers. The week following Macías's funeral, one-third of the nation's priests and one-sixth of its nuns signed a petition addressed to the pope, the Salvadoran bishops' conference, and the governments of Latin America beseeching them to do something to corral the military and the death squads. That's how desperate the situation had become.

Just a few days after Macías's death, Romero released his fourth and final pastoral letter. The very act of composing it reaffirmed his sense of solidarity with the people: Romero had sent out a questionnaire to clergy, base communities, and Church-sponsored charities requesting feedback on questions such as "What is our country's greatest sin?" and "Who is Jesus Christ for you?" The Church, he affirmed in his letter, was commissioned by God to be "the voice of the voiceless."[14] His questionnaire was one way of honoring that charge.

The fundamental purpose of the letter was to report the Puebla conference's conclusions about the responsibility of the Church in Latin America and particularly in El Salvador. The themes touched on in it were ones that Romero had voiced again and again since becoming archbishop: the preferential option for the poor, the virtue of nonviolence, and the proper relationship of faith to politics. But there was a more confident tone to his observations about social justice and a firmness in his repudiation of the "ideology of national security" and the "absolutization of idolatry of power" embraced by the Salvadoran government and oligarchy.[15] It was clear he had come into his own.

In keeping with the spirit of Puebla—as well as Vatican II, Paul VI's *Evangelii Nuntiandi,* and Medellín—the fundamental gift the Church had to offer El Salvador, wrote Romero, was simply to be itself by sharing the message of the Gospel "for the full salvation and betterment of men and women."[16] This meant denouncing individual and institutional evils which hampered that goal while promoting an integral humanism rooted in the Gospel that focused on both spiritual and material liberation. El Salvador needed personal conversion on the part of individuals and "profound structural changes in the social and political life." The Salvadoran Church's responsibility was to actively guide that transformation by preaching and modeling nonviolent resistance to injustice.[17] As Romero had noted in his third pastoral letter, peaceful strategies for fundamental change are anything but passive.

One of the ways to spread the Gospel message of nonviolent liberation is by empowering a "mass apostolate" of base communities and organizations that represent the interests of *campesinos.* Romero stressed, however, that devotion to Christ and the teachings of the Church is essential to this goal. Otherwise, the risk was too great of simply giving rise to even more political factions willing to use violence as a means to their end—a point that echoed Pope Paul's warning in his 1975 *Evangelii Nuntiandi*.

Again, none of this would have surprised readers of Romero's earlier pastoral letters. But in one regard, he *did* venture into new territory by devoting a section to Marxism. This was significant, since the standard government and oligarchic objection to *campesino* unionization or political dissent of any kind was that it was inspired by Communist ideology.

Although acknowledging that Marxism is a "complex concept" that can be used in ways destructive of human freedom and dignity, Romero argued it ought to be studied and clarified to see what in it, if anything, is compatible with the Church's mission— if for no other reason than, as the Puebla bishops pointed out, fear of it "keeps many from facing up to the oppressive reality of liberal capitalism." It's undoubtedly true that Marxism as a materialistic worldview that denies the existence of God and encourages class warfare is "diametrically opposed" to Christianity. But its "scientific analysis of the economic and social order" can be examined and evaluated independently of that worldview.[18] Marxist ideology, in other words, is dangerous and incompatible with the Gospel message. But if its methodology helps clarify the nature of economic inequality, it has its uses.

Despite Romero's public pleas to government officials and insurgents alike for a cessation of violence, the military continued ramping up its campaign against dissidents and rebels, energized by the July success of the Sandinista revolution in Nicaragua, responded in kind. By the end of September, at least sixty-five people had been disappeared and nearly six hundred murdered, four times more than in the previous year. Significantly, political arrests were down during that same period of time by more than half. This suggested a chilling fact: The government had dropped the pretense of legal procedure and gone straight to the murder of suspects. As Romero said in a mid-October homily after one of his friends, a *campesino* union leader, had been slaughtered, "The government has emptied the prisons of political prisoners, but unfortunately the cemeteries have filled with the dead."[19]

The chaos ripping El Salvador apart precipitated yet another change of government that same month. A group of army officers staged a bloodless coup that sent President Romero fleeing to Guatemala. The new junta, comprising two military officers and three civilians—the president of the Central American University, a leader of the political opposition, and a prominent businessman— promised land reform and a return to judicial process. Romero tentatively welcomed the change, choosing to give the leaders of the so-called "Young Officers Coup" the benefit of doubt. But despite the new leadership's political promises, violence accelerated throughout the rest of the year as the fledgling government struggled to survive long enough to actually begin the process of reform. It was as if discontent in the land had reached a tipping point that left no room for peaceful change.

Romero supported the junta longer than many thought he should have. One seminarian recalled that the bishop's friends were surprised and even shocked by his endorsement of it, and that a heated argument erupted between Romero and seminary students when they "threw it in his face" by telling him "straight out that he was giving his blessing to the military."[20] Others were even harsher in their recriminations. One group confronted him with the names and stories of children murdered by security forces, deliberately seeking to upset him. "We were really angry with Monseñor Romero because of his sympathy for the junta, and we wanted to make him feel it!"[21]

On October 29, a revolutionary group bearing the unwieldy name of People's League of February 28 rioted in the streets of San Salvador with the deliberate intention of provoking a showdown with the national guard. The ruckus ended with nearly two hundred civilians dead or wounded. Six hundred others, some of them League members holding a policeman hostage, crammed into a church seeking sanctuary. Guardsmen had surrounded the church, vowing vengeance unless the hostage was released, when Romero arrived on the scene in the hope of defusing the situation. On seeing him, the troop commander exploded in fury. "You!" he screamed at Romero. "It's your fault all this is happening! It's because of your idiotic sermons. So you can just step aside. You don't know shit about what's happening here!"[22]

Romero eventually managed to calm him down and successfully negotiated for the release of the hostage and safe passage for the protesters. But the bloodiness of the day soured him on the Young Officers Coup. Nonviolent though it had been, reformist as it promised to be, it failed to end the repression and was powerless to stop the killing.

Nor was Romero the only person disenchanted with the government. The military, which had supported the mid-October coup, now revolted and on December 18 assumed the nation's leadership. By the first day of 1980, the five men in the Young Officers Coup junta had resigned, placing the reins of power firmly in the hands of a new coalition made up of hard-line senior military officers and Christian Democrats. The United States, fearful of a Sandinista-like revolution in El Salvador unless the chaos was brought under control, threw its weight behind the new government and began feeding it money and weapons.

The forty-eighth anniversary of *la Matanza,* the 1932 peasant uprising in which thirty thousand *campesinos* had been slaughtered, fell on January 22, 1980. To commemorate it, and to show resistance to the new government, thousands of people processed through the streets of El Salvador, congregating in front of the National Palace. When they arrived, guardsmen began indiscriminately firing on them. Radio stations broadcast real-time descriptions of the carnage until the government cut their transmissions and imposed a complete radio blackout for the next forty-eight hours.

In his homily that Sunday, a shaken Romero spoke of the tragedy both defiantly and hopefully.

> The people's cry for liberation is a shout that rises up to God and that nothing and no one can now stop. When some fall in the struggle, provided it be with sincere love for the people and in search of a true liberation, we should consider them always present among us—not only because they stay in the memory of those who continue their struggles, but also because the transcendence of our faith teaches us that the body's destruction does not end human life.[23]

In just two months Romero would fall in the struggle.

CHAPTER TEN

Death Comes for the Archbishop

"The greatest sign of faith in a God of life is the witness of
those who are ready to give up their own life."[1]

The *la Matanza* anniversary massacre delayed a trip to Belgium
that had been in the works for some time. Romero had been
awarded another honorary degree, this one from the Catholic
University of Louvain, and he planned to travel to Belgium to
receive it.

Departing El Salvador for Louvain in late January 1980,
Romero stopped over in his beloved Rome for a couple of days to
meet with John Paul II. It was the final time he would see either
the pope or the city he'd fallen in love with as a young seminarian.

Romero's meeting with the pope went better than his previous
one. Instead of being deflated by the pope's scolding, Romero
stood his ground when John Paul once again warned him to be
more circumspect in his challenge to the government lest he be
seen as a Communist sympathizer. Romero replied that while he
appreciated the pope's counsel, preaching anti-Communism in El
Salvador was risky because it was the battle cry of the very government and oligarchy that oppressed the people. As Romero remembered the discussion afterward, John Paul conceded the point and
gave him "a fraternal embrace" at the end of the audience.[2]

Romero's meeting the next day with Vatican secretary of state Cardinal Agostino Casaroli revealed why the pope had warned him against appearing to sympathize with the Salvadoran left. An official from the US State Department had made an unofficial complaint about Romero to the secretariat, alleging that his criticism of the Salvadoran government was playing into the hands of Marxist militants and their sympathizers. President Jimmy Carter, alarmed by the socialist revolution that overthrew the Somoza regime in Nicaragua, had been shipping gas masks and bullet-proof vests to Salvador in a material show of support for the new military junta. The outspoken archbishop of San Salvador was getting in the way of US foreign policy.

Romero defended his actions to Casaroli with the same firmness he'd shown in his audience with the pope. He reiterated that preaching against Communism risked the danger of being identified with the Salvadoran elite, "who talk of anticommunism not in order to defend Christian principles, but rather to defend their materialistic interests." But he also assured the cardinal that he shared the Vatican's worry about the popular liberation movement falling prey to "foreign ideologies."[3] This may have been a sly double entendre on Romero's part. Given the US government's support of the junta, one suspects it wasn't only Soviet meddling in his nation's domestic affairs that worried the archbishop.

Romero flew directly to Belgium from Rome on February 2 to receive his degree. The speech he gave in accepting it was one of the finest of his life.

He confessed that he was an expert in neither politics nor theology, and so couldn't offer his Louvain audience a learned theoretical discourse on the proper relationship between faith and politics. Instead, he told them, he wished to speak "simply as a pastor" whose experience in El Salvador had taught him "the beautiful but harsh truth" that Christian faith means getting involved in the world rather than retreating from it. "The church is not a fortress set apart from the city," he said. Instead, it "follows Jesus who lived, worked, battled and died in the midst of a city."[4]

Part of that beautiful but harsh truth, Romero continued, is the rejection of a "false universalism" that too often in the past has allied the Church with the powerful and rich. Romero's personal ministry to those robbed by the wealthy and oppressed by unjust political institutions demonstrated to him that "the sublimity of Christian love ought to be mediated through the overriding necessity of justice for the majority" rather than the privileged minority. Consequently, one of the Church's tasks was to empower the poor to take an active role in their own liberation. The old days of "ecclesiastical paternalism" must end.[5]

Christians, said Romero, "believe in a living God who gives life to men and women and wants them truly to live." Therefore, the choice that all Christians face is simple: "to be in favor of life or to be in favor of death." When it comes to El Salvador or any other nation in which systematic injustice against the poor is practiced, "neutrality is impossible" for the Christian. And then Romero uttered a sentence which, tragically, turned out to be a portend of his own future: "The greatest sign of faith in a God of life is the witness of those who are ready to give up their own life."[6]

On his return to El Salvador, Romero began drafting a letter he intended to send to President Carter. It was motivated by the State Department's complaint to the Vatican Secretariat of State, but also by breaking newspaper reports that US military aid to the junta had gone way beyond defensive antiriot gear to the tune of nearly six million dollars in weapons. The munition shipments would be accompanied by US advisors who would train Salvadoran security forces in their tactical use.

Romero began his letter by reminding Carter that he was a publicly professed born-again Christian and champion of human rights—gentle nudges that invited the president to ask himself if his planned aid to the Salvadoran government was consistent with who he said he was. He went on to express his concerns that the aid would do nothing to quell unrest in his country, but on the contrary would exacerbate it. Consequently, he asked Carter to guarantee that his administration wouldn't try to manipulate Salvador with military aid or economic and diplomatic pressure that could only inflict more hardship on the nation's most vulnerable citizens. Salvadorans, he concluded, were the only ones morally authorized to solve their own problems.

Knowing that the letter was likely to die a silent death if all he did was send it through the usual diplomatic channels, Romero decided to go public with it. He read it at his Sunday homily, broadcast to the entire nation, on February 17.

The responses were immediate and predictable. Salvadoran *campesinos*, unionists, and government resisters were overjoyed at Romero's defiance of Carter. The Salvadoran government, oligarchy, and bishops—minus Romero's steady ally Rivera—were incensed. The US State Department lodged an angry complaint with the Vatican—this time an official one—and a diplomat from the US embassy in El Salvador visited Romero to defend his government's policy. A month later, Secretary of State Cyrus Vance, trying to control the situation, wrote to Romero personally to assure him that the US had no intention of interfering in El Salvador's domestic affairs. But Romero knew better. As he noted in his diary the day after he publicly read his own letter,

US military aid to El Salvador had introduced the "new concept of special warfare which consists in eliminating in a murderous way all the efforts of the popular organizations, using the pretext of communion or terrorism." This special warfare justified the wholesale killing of entire families who, "according to this theory, are totally poisoned by these terrorist concepts and must be eliminated."[7] It's a way of waging war, in other words, that is utterly immoral under any circumstances.

The day after Romero read his letter in the cathedral, the diocesan YSAX radio station's transmitter was blown up. The attack was obviously intended to silence Romero's voice, but it didn't succeed. The following Sunday, a Costa Rican shortwave station recorded and broadcast his homily throughout all of Latin America. In a welcome bit of poetic justice, the sabotage of YSAX increased rather than lessened Romero's audience.

Less than a month later, another bomb that would have caused untold havoc had it exploded fortunately failed to go off. On March 9, Romero celebrated a funeral Mass for Mario Zamora, a left-wing political leader who had been murdered by a death squad. The church where the funeral was held was packed with mourners, supporters, dozens of party leaders, and journalists. The service concluded without incident. But the next morning, a suitcase containing seventy-two dynamite sticks was discovered in the church. For some reason, the homemade bomb's triggering mechanism, timed to detonate during the Mass, had failed. Otherwise the church and surrounding blocks would have been decimated, most likely taking Romero and everyone else at Zamora's funeral with them.

It wasn't the first time Romero's life had been threatened. In fact, he had received so many death threats during his final months as archbishop that he sometimes found them more distracting than frightening. But he was never free of the unsettling awareness that he was a target, and during his last weeks, as his spiritual advisor later revealed, he suffered greatly from dread of violent death. Even then, however, he was worried about innocent bystanders who might be victimized by an attack on his person. Once scolded by a well-wisher for venturing out in the city and countryside by himself, Romero replied, "I prefer it this way. When what I'm expecting to happen, happens, I want to be alone, so it's only me they get. I don't want anyone else to suffer."[8]

The prospect of his own murder was less troubling to him than the violence against "enemies of the state" that was increasing by leaps and bounds. In January 1980, an average of ten daily verified assassinations occurred throughout El Salvador. In all likelihood, the actual number of violent deaths was higher. February saw the number of verified daily murders jump to fifteen. In March, there was yet another increase. And in the aftermath of Romero's own martyrdom, the killing escalated to such an extent that the civil war he had feared for so long became a grim reality. In the first two years following his death, 35,000 Salvadorans perished; another 40,000 would die before the war finally ended in 1992. Thousands more simply disappeared, their bodies hastily buried in mass graves or dropped into the ocean. Fifteen percent of the nation's population fled to escape the incessant violence. A United Nations Truth Commission later concluded that 85 percent of the recorded deaths were at the hands of the Salvadoran security forces and clandestine death squads. Shamefully, the Salvadoran prelates, with the sole exception of Bishop Rivera, continued to support the repressive government and oligarchy whose excesses caused most of the mayhem. They acted as if the Medellín and

Puebla conferences—or, for that matter, Romero—had never existed.

In the final week of Romero's life violence accelerated at a dizzying rate. Terrified *campesinos* fled from security forces rampaging through the countryside to refugee centers that the archbishop had established in San Salvador. Parish rectories and churches were shaken down by national guardsmen in search of subversives, which by this time included anyone who had ever voiced reservations about the government or who simply was the target of a personal grudge by an ORDEN member. In a couple of rural hamlets, children were slaughtered alongside their parents. Union halls and retreat centers were raided by the police. Armed resistance groups retaliated, sometimes with merciless ferocity.

As he had always done, Romero deplored and publicly called out the violence perpetrated by both sides. Having to do so again and again with no observable success must have been emotionally and spiritually exhausting. No matter how hard he tried, nothing seemed to be effective against the growing tide of terror that was transforming El Salvador into a police state. Still, he persevered. "The denouncements of the left against the right and the hatred of the right for the left appear irreconcilable, and those in the middle say, wherever the violence comes from, be tough on them both," he noted in one of his final homilies. "There can be no love at all where people take sides to the point of hating others. We need to burst these dikes, we need to feel that there is a Father who loves us all and awaits us all. We need to learn to pray the Our Father and tell him: Forgive us as we forgive."[9]

That year, the fifth Sunday in Lent fell on March 23. Technicians and engineers had been scrambling ever since YSAX's transmitter was bombed to get the radio station back up and running, and they finally finished the job just in time to broadcast Romero's homily that day. It would be his last recorded sermon.

In it, Romero said that the Salvadoran Church's mission was to open up God's Word for all people, both the oppressed and the oppressor, in order to shed light on the social, political, and economic realities challenging the nation. He repeated what he had said so often: Such a task wasn't an unwarranted meddling in politics, but a proclamation of the Easter promise of Christianity—that despite the cruelties of injustice and poverty, the prospect of justice with peace endured. "No one can extinguish the life that Christ resurrected. Not even death and hatred against Him and against His Church will be able to overcome it. Christ is the victor!"

This Easter promise, Romero told his listeners, is what sustained him in the midst of the horrors occurring in El Salvador. "I ask the Lord during the week, while I gather the people's cries and the sorrow stemming from so much crime, the ignominy of so much violence, to give me the fitting word to console, to denounce, to call to repentance."

Romero reminded everyone that liberation doesn't come magically and certainly not by violence, but only through fidelity to Jesus Christ and actions based upon his teachings and example. Then he said something that electrified everyone listening to him, friends and foes alike, and which even today stirs the heart. In all likelihood, it was the final straw for his enemies, who killed him the next day.

> I would like to appeal in a special way to the army's enlisted men, and in particular to the ranks of the national guard and the police—those in the barracks. Brothers: you are part of our own people. You kill your

own *campesino* brothers and sisters. And before an order to kill that a man may give, God's law must prevail that says: Thou shalt not kill! No soldier is obliged to obey an order against the law of God. No one has to fulfill an immoral law. It is time to take back your consciences and to obey your consciences rather than the orders of sin. The Church, defender of the rights of God, of the law of God, of human dignity, of the person, cannot remain silent before such abomination. We want the government to understand seriously that reforms are worth nothing if they are stained with so much blood. In the name of God, and in the name of this suffering people, whose laments rise to heaven each day more tumultuous, I beg you, I beseech you, I order you in the name of God: Stop the repression![10]

Romero's words were interrupted five times by enthusiastic applause. Many of those who heard his homily later praised it as the most powerful one he'd ever given. The intensity with which he delivered it drained Romero physically and emotionally. But it energized his listeners, inspiring those committed to the struggle for liberation and human rights, enraging those in favor of the status quo, and goading both groups to action.

When Mass was concluded, and after he'd endured a long press conference, an exhausted Romero went to the home of his old friend Salvador Barraza to unwind. The family remembered that he was uncharacteristically subdued and melancholy. He even wept a little. At the time, the Barrazas chalked his mood up to weariness. In hindsight, it seemed to have been a foreboding of what awaited the archbishop on the following day.

On Monday, March 24, Romero was scheduled to celebrate a 6:00 p.m. Mass for the first anniversary of the death of a friend's mother. It was to be held in the chapel of the cancer hospital on whose grounds he lived. Shortly before the Mass, Romero surprised Barraza by spontaneously asking if he would drive him to see his confessor.

The appointed readings for the Mass focused on death and resurrection: Christ risen from the dead (1 Corinthians 15:20–28), Psalm 23's assurance that God walks with us in the valley of the shadow of death, and the necessity for a grain of wheat to fall to the earth and die before it can bear fruit (John 12:23–26). In his brief homily, Romero told the gathered people that "one must not love oneself so much as to avoid getting involved in the risks of life that history demands of us." No act of Christian sacrifice is in vain. In imitation of the sacrifice offered at each Eucharist, may all Christians, Romero prayed, "give our body and our blood to suffering and pain—like Christ, not for self, but to bring about justice and peace for our people."[11]

And then it was over. Three years and twelve days from that nightmarish afternoon when Rutilio Grande was gunned down, the grain of wheat which was Oscar Romero fell to the earth and died. A single rifle shot hit him squarely in the chest as he stood at the altar. He collapsed, blood streaming from his mouth and nose, as horrified nuns ran to his assistance. It's not entirely clear if he died on the chapel floor or in the emergency room to which he was taken. But in fewer than ten minutes, Romero was gone.

It was only a few days later that Salvadorans, stunned by his murder, began to take notice of something Romero had told a Mexican reporter two weeks earlier. Admitting that his life was in constant danger, Romero said, "I must tell you, as a Christian, I do not believe in death without resurrection. If I am killed, I shall arise in the Salvadoran people. I say so without boasting, with the greatest humility.... A bishop will die, but God's church, which is the people, will never die."[12]

Romero's funeral Mass was celebrated on Palm Sunday. Bishops from around the world as well as dozens of representatives from Protestant denominations traveled to San Salvador to pay their final respects. Some three hundred Salvadoran priests concelebrated, as did noted Peruvian liberation theologian Gustavo Gutiérrez. But there was an absence among the assembled mourners glaringly obvious to everyone: With the exception of Rivera, none of the Salvadoran bishops attended. Aparicio, Alvarez, Barrera, and Revelo chose to sit the funeral out as a final show of disrespect to the man they had tirelessly vilified and obstructed when he was alive.

The altar and Romero's coffin were set up outside the cathedral entrance in sight of the thousands of mourners who came from all parts of El Salvador to say goodbye to Romero. But the farewell was disrupted in the middle of the funeral homily. A bomb exploded in the cathedral plaza, followed by indiscriminate gunfire that seemed to come from the direction of the National Palace. To this day it's uncertain whether government or rebel forces initiated the chaos that ensued.

As soon as the shots were fired, the assembled crowd panicked and began running helter-skelter. Then another explosion blasted through the already frenzied crowd. In the confusion, at least forty people were trampled to death and children were separated from their parents. James Connor, an American Jesuit, remembered how "a little peasant girl named Reina, dressed up in her brown-and-white checked Sunday dress, clung to me in desperation and pleaded, 'Padre.'"[13] Hundreds of terrified men, women, and children crammed into the cathedral seeking sanctuary.

Realizing that the outdoor liturgy could not be resumed, the principal celebrant and a few priests managed to get Romero's coffin inside the cathedral, where they hastily laid his body to rest in the crypt prepared for him. There was no Eucharist; wine and hosts on the open-air altar had been spilled and scattered in the chaos caused by the explosions. Nor was a missal to hand. So the bishop of Chiapas pulled a small devotional from his pocket, and used a few prayers from it to send Archbishop Romero on his way home.

People around the world, shaken by the death of a man many were already calling a saint, were horrified once again at the senseless violence that disrupted his funeral. Why, they asked, would God have allowed such a terrible thing to happen? But Gustavo Gutiérrez, who wondered that himself, came to this conclusion:

> Could Monseñor Romero, who wanted to give his life for his people, have been buried in a kind of oasis of peace? Many of us asked ourselves that question, almost discreetly, as we buried him two hours after being enclosed in the cathedral. Could he have been buried in isolation from the reality that his people lived daily?
>
> Unfortunately, it could not have been otherwise. Monseñor Romero's burial took place in the midst of the suffering and struggles of his people.[14]

"In the midst of his people"—the *campesinos* whom Romero loved and championed during his final three years, the people who baptized him and for whose sake he willingly offered up his life.

NOTES

EPIGRAPH

1. Oscar Romero, homily, "His Kingdom Will Have No End," November 26, 1978.

INTRODUCTION

1. Oscar Romero, *The Church Cannot Remain Silent: Unpublished Letters and Other Writings,* trans. Gene Palumbo and Dinah Livingstone (Maryknoll, NY: Orbis, 2016), 26.
2. Maria Lopez Vigil, *Monseñor Romero: Memories in Mosaic,* trans. Kathy Ogle (Maryknoll, NY: Orbis, 2013), 294.
3. Oscar Romero, *The Violence of Love,* ed. and trans. James Brockman (Maryknoll, NY: Orbis / Farmington, PA: Plough, 2004), 197.
4. Oscar Romero, *Voice of the Voiceless, The Four Pastoral Letters and Other Statements,* trans. Michael J. Walsh (Maryknoll, NY: Orbis, 1985), 180–181.
5. Oscar Romero, "Three Christian Forces for Liberation," November 11, 1979. Archbishop Oscar Romero Trust.
6. Jon Sobrino, *Archbishop Romero: Memories and Reflections,* trans. Robert R. Barr, J. Matthew Ashley, Margaret Wilde. Revised Edition (Maryknoll, NY: Orbis, 2016), 40.

CHAPTER ONE

1. Vigil, 3.
2. Sobrino, 52.
3. Vigil, 3.
4. Vigil, 3–4.
5. Vigil, 3.
6. Vigil, 4.
7. Will, 21.
8. Jeffrey L. Gould and Aldo A. Lauria-Santiago, *To Rise in Darkness: Revolution, Repression, and Memory in El Salvador, 1920-1932* (Durham, NC: Duke University Press, 2008), 20.
9. Jeffrey M. Paige, *Coffee and Power: Revolution and the Rise of Democracy in Central America* (Cambridge, MA: Harvard University Press, 1997),103.

CHAPTER TWO

1. James Brockman, *Romero: A Life* (Maryknoll, NY: Orbis, 1989), 39.
2. Roberto Morozzo della Rocca, *Oscar Romero: Prophet of Hope*, trans. Michael J. Miller (London: Darton, Longman and Todd, Ltd., 2015), 7-8.
3. Morozzo della Rocca, 7–8.
4. John Paul II; Francis, section 93.
5. Morozzo della Rocca, 7.
6. Brockman, 37.
7. Brockman, 38.
8. Morozzo della Rocca, 7.
9. Brockman, 39.
10. Vigil, 5.
11. Brockman, 38.

CHAPTER THREE

1. Romero, *The Church Cannot Remain Silent*, 67.
2. Vigil, 6.
3. Emily Wade Will, *Archbishop Oscar Romero: The Making of a Martyr* (Eugene, OR: Resource / Wipf and Stock, 2016), 42.
4. Vigil, 10.
5. Vigil, 7.
6. Vigil, 6.
7. Vigil, 16.
8. John XXIII, "Opening Address to the Vatican II Council," October 11, 1962.
9. Morozzo della Rocca, 23.
10. Vigil, 16.

CHAPTER FOUR

1. Vigil, 34.
2. Vigil, 30–31.
3. Vigil, 17.
4. Penny Lernoux, *Cry of the People* (Garden City, NY: Doubleday, 1980), 37.
5. Medellín Conference, final document, September 6, 1968.
6. Pablo Galdamez. *Faith of a People: The Life of a Basic Christian Community in El Salvador.* (Maryknoll, NY: Orbis, 1986).
7. Morozzo della Rocca, 39.

8. Vigil, 25.
9. Vigil, 26, 27.
10. Vigil, 29.
11. Rhina Guidos, *Rutilio Grande: A Table for All* (Collegeville, MN: Liturgical, 2018), 57.
12. Brockman, 49.
13. Vigil, 34.

CHAPTER FIVE
1. Vigil, 42.
2. Romero, 50.
3. Vigil, 41.
4. Kevin Clarke, *Oscar Romero: Love Must Win Out* (Collegeville, MN: Liturgical, 2014), 65.
5. Will, 83–84.
6. Vigil, 41.
7. *Evangelii Nuntiandi,* 58.
8. *Evangelii Nuntiandi,* 58.
9. *Evangelii Nuntiandi,* 31.
10. Brockman, 56–57.
11. Vigil, 45.
12. Vigil, 42.
13. Will, 90.

CHAPTER SIX
1. Vigil, 78.
2. Vigil, 51.
3. Vigil, 62.
4. Brockman, 8.
5. Thomas M. Kelly, *Rutilio Grande, SJ: Homilies and Writings* (Collegeville, MN: Liturgical, 2015), 120.
6. Sobrino, 9.
7. Sobrino, 6–7.
8. Oscar Romero, "The One Mass," March 20, 1977. Archbishop Oscar Romero Trust.
9. Morozzo della Rocca, 81.
10. Sobrino, 7.
11. Vigil, 78.

Chapter Seven

1. Oscar Romero, "The Mystery of Christ," June 19, 1977. Archbishop Oscar Romero Trust.
2. Vigil, 106.
3. Vigil, 106.
4. Vigil, 109.
5. Romero, *Voice of the Voiceless,* 54.
6. Romero, *Voice of the Voiceless,* 57.
7. Romero, *Voice of the Voiceless,* 59.
8. Romero, *Voice of the Voiceless,* 61.
9. Oscar Romero, "The Church's Mission," May 8, 1977. Archbishop Oscar Romero Trust.
10. Oscar Romero, "An Ideal that Doesn't Die," May 12, 1977. Archbishop Oscar Romero Trust.
11. Brockman, 31.
12. Vigil, 117.
13. Romero, "The Mystery of Christ."
14. Romero, "The Mystery of Christ."
15. Vigil, 118.
16. Romero, *Voice of the Voiceless,* 68.
17. Romero, *Voice of the Voiceless,* 77.
18. Romero, *Voice of the Voiceless,* 77.
19. Romero, *Voice of the Voiceless,* 78.
20. Romero, *Voice of the Voiceless,* 82.
21. Romero, *Voice of the Voiceless,* 83.
22. Oscar Romero, "The Right Use of the Goods God Created," September 25, 1977. Archbishop Oscar Romero Trust.
23. Vigil, 124.
24. Vigil, 124, 125.
25. Romero, "The Church of Hope," November 27, 1977.
26. Romero, *The Church Cannot Remain Silent,* 18.

Chapter Eight

1. Oscar Romero, *A Shepherd's Diary,* trans. Irene B. Hodgson (Cincinnati: St. Anthony Messenger Press, 1993), 24.
2. Romero, *Voice of the Voiceless,* 162.
3. Romero, *Voice of the Voiceless,* 163.
4. Romero, *Voice of the Voiceless,* 164.

5. Romero, *Voice of the Voiceless*, 165.
6. Brockman, 110.
7. Brockman, 110.
8. Romero, *A Shepherd's Diary*, 24.
9. Romero, *A Shepherd's Diary*, 23, 26, 27.
10. Oscar Romero, "Pentecost, the Church's Birthday," May 14, 1978. Archbishop Oscar Romero Trust.
11. Romero, *A Shepherd's Diary*, 66.
12. Romero, *A Shepherd's Diary*, 69.
13. Romero, *A Shepherd's Diary*, 69.
14. Romero, *A Shepherd's Diary*, 77.
15. Romero, *Voice of the Voiceless*, 86.
16. Romero, *Voice of the Voiceless*, 97.
17. Romero, *Voice of the Voiceless*, 99.
18. Romero, *Voice of the Voiceless*, 108, 109.
19. Romero, *Voice of the Voiceless*, 109.
20. Brockman, 146.
21. Romero, *A Shepherd's Diary*, 84.
22. Brockman, 178.

CHAPTER NINE
1. Romero, in Brockman, 161.
2. Vigil, 187.
3. Oscar Romero, "An Assassination that Speaks of Resurrection," January 21, 1979. Archbishop Oscar Romero Trust.
4. Clarke, 117.
5. Romero, *A Shepherd's Diary*, 176.
6. Wright, 93.
7. Brockman, 161.
8. Brockman, 172.
9. Oscar Romero, "The Voice of Blood," June 21, 1979.
10. Romero, *A Shepherd's Diary*, 211.
11. Romero, *A Shepherd's Diary*, 214.
12. Romero, *A Shepherd's Diary*, 215.
13. Vigil, 213–216.
14. Romero, *Voice of the Voiceless*, 138.
15. Romero, *Voice of the Voiceless*, 122.
16. Romero, *Voice of the Voiceless*, 128.

17. Romero, *Voice of the Voiceless*, 138.
18. Romero, *Voice of the Voiceless*, 146.
19. Oscar Romero, "Three Conditions to Enter the Kingdom of God," October 14, 1979. Archbishop Oscar Romero Trust.
20. Vigil, 233.
21. Vigil, 236.
22. Vigil, 239.
23. Oscar Romero, "The Homily, Living Presence of God's Word," January 27, 1980. Archbishop Oscar Romero Trust.

CHAPTER TEN
1. Romero, *Voice of the Voiceless*, 185.
2. Romero, *A Shepherd's Diary*, 465.
3. Romero, *A Shepherd's Diary*, 468.
4. Romero, *Voice of the Voiceless*, 178.
5. Romero, *Voice of the Voiceless*, 185.
6. Romero, *Voice of the Voiceless*, 185.
7. Romero, *A Shepherd's Diary*, 493.
8. Vigil, 270.
9. Oscar Romero, "Reconciliation in Christ, True Liberation," March 16, 1980. Archbishop Oscar Romero Trust.
10. Oscar Romero, "The Church in the Service of Personal, Community and Transcendent Liberation," March 23, 1980. Archbishop Oscar Romero Trust.
11. Oscar Romero, "Final Homily," March 24, 1980. Archbishop Oscar Romero Trust.
12. Brockman, 248.
13. Connor, "A Report from Romero's Funeral"
14. Dennis, Golden, and Wright, 104.

Armstrong, Robert and Janet Shenk, *El Salvador: The Face of Revolution.* Boston, MA: South End, 1982.

Brockman, James R. *Romero: A Life.* Maryknoll, NY: Orbis, 1989.

Clarke, Kevin. *Oscar Romero: Love Must Win Out.* Collegeville, MN: Liturgical, 2014.

Connor, James L. "A Report from Romero's Funeral." *America,* April 26, 1980, https://www.americamagazine.org/issue/100/report-romeros-funeral.

Dennis, Marie, Renny Golden, and Scott Wright, *Oscar Romero: Reflections on his Life and Writings.* Maryknoll, NY: Orbis, 2000.

Francis. *Laudato Si'.* Huntington, IN: Our Sunday Visitor, 2015.

Galdámez, Pablo. *Faith of a People: The Life of a Basic Christian Community in El Salvador.* Maryknoll, NY: Orbis, 1986.

Gould, Jeffrey L. and Aldo A. Lauria-Santiago, *To Rise in Darkness: Revolution, Repression, and Memory in El Salvador, 1920–1932.* Durham, NC: Duke University Press, 2008.

Guidos, Rhina. *Rutilio Grande: A Table for All.* Collegeville, MN: Liturgical, 2018.

John XXIII. "Opening Address to the Vatican II Council." October 11, 1962, https://www.catholicculture.org/culture/library/view.cfm?recnum=3233.

John Paul II. "Address to Indigenous and Rural People," Cuilapan, Mexico. January 29, 1979, https://w2.vatican.va/content/john-paul ii/en/speeches/1979/january/documents/hf_jpii_spe_19790129_ messico-cuilapan-indios.html.

Kelly, Thomas M. *Rutilio Grande, SJ: Homilies and Writings.* Collegeville, MN: Liturgical, 2015.

Lernoux, Penny. *Cry of the People.* Garden City, NY: Doubleday, 1980.

Marrin, Pat. "Oscar Romero Sainthood Cause on Long, Tangled Path." *National Catholic Reporter,* May 10, 2013, https://www.ncronline.org/news/people/oscar-romero-sainthood-cause-long-tangled-path.

Medellín Conference. Final Document, 6 September 1968, http://www.geraldschlabach.net/Medellin-1968-excerpts/.

Morozzo della Rocca, Roberto. *Oscar Romero: Prophet of Hope*, trans. Michael J. Miller. London: Darton, Longman and Todd, 2015.

Paige, Jeffrey M. *Coffee and Power: Revolution and the Rise of Democracy in Central America*. Cambridge, MA: Harvard University Press, 1997.

Paul VI, On Evangelization in the Modern World *(Evangelii Nuntiandi)*. Boston, MA: Pauline, 1975.

Romero, Oscar. *A Shepherd's Diary*, trans. Irene B. Hodgson. Cincinnati: St. Anthony Messenger Press, 1993.

_____. "An Assassination that Speaks of Resurrection," January 21, 1979. Archbishop Oscar Romero Trust, http://www.romerotrust.org.uk/homilies-and-writings/homilies/assassination-speaks-resurrection.

_____. "An Ideal that Doesn't Die," May 12, 1977. Archbishop Oscar Romero Trust, http://www.romerotrust.org.uk/homilies-and-writings/homilies/ideal-doesnt-die.

_____. *The Church Cannot Remain Silent: Unpublished Letters and Other Writings*, trans. Gene Palumbo and Dinah Livingstone. Maryknoll, NY: Orbis, 2016.

_____. "The Church in the Service of Personal, Community and Transcendent Liberation," March 23, 1980. Archbishop Oscar Romero Trust, http://www.romerotrust.org.uk/homilies-and-writings/homilies/church-service-personal-community-and-transcendent-liberation.

_____. "The Church of Hope," November 27, 1977. Archbishop Oscar Romero Trust, http://www.romerotrust.org.uk/homilies-and-writings/homilies/church-hope.

_____. "The Church's Mission," May 8, 1977. Archbishop Oscar Romero Trust, http://www.romerotrust.org.uk/homilies-and-writings/homilies/churchs-mission.

_____. "Final Homily," March 24, 1980. Archbishop Oscar Romero Trust, http://www.romerotrust.org.uk/homilies-and-writings/homilies/final-homily-archbishop-romero.

_____. "His Kingdom Will Have No End," November 26, 1978. Archbishop Oscar Romero Trust, http://www.romerotrust.org.uk/homilies-and-writings/homilies/his-kingdom-will-have-no-end.

_____. *Homilies, 1977-1980*. The Archbishop Oscar Romero Trust, http://www.romerotrust.org.uk/.

_____. "The Homily, Living Presence of God's Word," January 27, 1980. Archbishop OscarRomero Trust., http://www.romerotrust.org.uk/

homilies-and-writings/homilies/homily-living-presence-gods-word.

_____. "The Mystery of Christ," June 19, 1977. Archbishop Oscar Romero Trust, http://www.romerotrust.org.uk/homilies-and-writings/ homilies/mystery-christ.

_____. "The One Mass," March 20, 1977. Archbishop Oscar Romero Trust, http://www.romerotrust.org.uk/homilies-and-writings/ homilies/one-mass.

_____. "Pentecost, the Church's Birthday," May 14, 1978. Archbishop Oscar Romero Trust, http://www.romerotrust.org.uk/ homilies-and-writings/homilies/pentecost-churchs-birthday.

_____. "The Right Use of the Goods God Created." Archbishop Oscar Romero Trust, http://www.romerotrust.org.uk/ homilies-and-writings/homilies/right-use-goods-god- created.

_____. "Three Christian Forces for Liberation," November 11, 1979. Archbishop Oscar Romero Trust, http://www.romerotrust.org.uk/ homilies-and-writings/homilies/three-christian-forces-liberation.

_____. "Three Conditions to Enter the Kingdom of God," October 14, 1979. Archbishop Oscar Romero Trust., http://www.romerotrust.org. uk/homilies-and-writings/homilies/three-conditions-enter-kingdom-god.

_____. *The Violence of Love*, ed. and trans. James Brockman. Maryknoll, NY: Orbis /Farmington, PA: Plough , 2004.

_____. "The Voice of Blood," June 21, 1979. Archbishop Oscar Romero Trust, http://www.romerotrust.org.uk/homilies-and-writings/ homilies/voice-blood.

_____. *Voice of the Voiceless: The Four Pastoral Letters and Other Statements,* trans. Michael J. Walsh. Maryknoll, NY: Orbis, 1985.

Sobrino, Jon. *Archbishop Romero: Memories and Reflections,* trans. Robert R. Barr, J. Matthew Ashley, Margaret Wilde. Revised Edition. Maryknoll, NY: Orbis, 2016.

Vigil, Maria Lopez. *Monseñor Romero: Memories in Mosaic,* trans. Kathy Ogle. Maryknoll, NY: Orbis, 2013.

Will, Emily Wade. *Archbishop Oscar Romero: The Making of a Martyr.* Eugene, OR: Resource / Wipf and Stock, 2016.

Wright, Scott. *Oscar Romero and the Communion of Saints.* Maryknoll, NY: Orbis, 2009.

ABOUT THE AUTHOR

KERRY WALTERS is a professor emeritus of philosophy and peace and justice studies at Gettysburg College in Pennsylvania. He is a prolific author whose books include *Saint Teresa of Calcutta: Missionary, Mother, Mystic; Practicing Presence: The Spirituality of Caring in Everyday Life;* and *The Art of Dying and Living.*